Back to the Garden

GROWING IN SPIRITUAL INTIMACY THROUGH PRAYER WITH YOUR SPOUSE

JAN MITCHELL, MSW
WAYNE MITCHELL, PhD

WESTBOW®
PRESS
A DIVISION OF THOMAS NELSON
& ZONDERVAN

WestBow Press books may be ordered through booksellers or by contacting:

WestBow Press
A Division of Thomas Nelson & Zondervan
1663 Liberty Drive
Bloomington, IN 47403
www.westbowpress.com
1 (866) 928-1240

ISBN: 978-1-4908-3607-2 (sc)
ISBN: 978-1-4908-3606-5 (e)

Library of Congress Control Number: 2014908177

Printed in the United States of America.

WestBow Press rev. date: 10/02/2014

Contents

Preface

The impetus to write a Christian workbook for couples desiring intimate prayer together came initially in the form of seeds planted by God in our own beginnings as a couple. God brought us together through a small Christian prayer group, and He continued to manifest Himself in our relationship through ongoing intimate prayer together. The actual story of our coming together is a script full of His writing, including why He chose to unite us in marriage at what seemed to be a too-late date and a too-late season.

We were both very aware that our marriage, by His design, was for the purpose of using us in marriage to magnify and glorify His name in some special way that was totally beyond what either of us could have imagined or done alone or apart from each other within our marriage. While our story could be a book in itself, suffice it to say that God has given us the privilege of knowing true spiritual intimacy as a couple in prayer, and it is far deeper and more emotionally satisfying than any physical intimacy we could have achieved.

We have been struck over the years by two things that must surely grieve God, the author of intimacy, regarding marriage. One observation—based on our own experiences of over forty adult years in churches, and the consensus of those in our small couples groups—is that the church as an institution does not appear to widely promote or equip married couples to come together alone in intimate prayer exclusively for each other.

We started and facilitated several small couples groups and discovered that only non-intimate needs would (or should) be openly prayed about in front of others. There were spouses who were not comfortable praying in front of their mate in a group. Instead, for deep and intimate concerns, a person would often go to a trusted friend for prayer and emotional support rather than to his or her spouse. More often than not, women and men formed separate prayer groups, often as part of a Bible study, where they received support and prayer apart from their mates.

While that may be appropriate in some instances, it separates spouses and robs them of the opportunity to experience all that God has for them as a couple through praying intimately together. These groups showed us a need for encouraging and equipping couples to pray together in private, as spiritual transparency in prayer requires privacy, just as physical baring before each other does. It is our own experience—as well as that reported by couples we surveyed who completed this book—that when spiritual intimacy in prayer is achieved with our spouses, we are surprised by God's presence and His heart for us and our marriage. This spiritual intimacy draws us lovingly toward both our Father and our mate, as we praise Him and petition Him on our mate's behalf. We can experience an overwhelming sense of love when joining together in intimacy with God in prayer. This can go far beyond the bounds of what man and wife can achieve through their physical union, no matter how satisfying that level of relationship may be.

The other observation—generalized from initially surveying both couples and church pastors that we knew personally—is that the majority of Christian couples did not pray together either often or intimately. Pastors we interviewed estimated that as many as 80 percent or more of the married couples in their respective churches did not pray together as a couple in their homes other than at meal times, if then. Couples who have shared with us their prayer habits, as well as their desires to experience greater spiritual intimacy in prayer together, confirmed this estimate. Even pastors with very godly and solid marriages have confessed to us that they did not pray deeply and solely with and for their spouses. In the process of gathering data and information regarding married couples and their prayer life patterns, we saw an expressed desire to experience intimate, confidential prayer as a couple—and the reasons that prevented it.

During three years of serious preparation for the first draft of this book, which included the gathering of lengthy, written surveys, three barriers emerged. (The original survey used is in Appendix 1, which can be a helpful tool for you and your spouse to use in assessing your own desire for and obstacles to intimate couple prayer.) The first barrier was a lack of knowledge, which was the initial impetus for writing this book. We were literally asked to write an instruction manual by the wife of one of the couples in our Bible study/prayer group.

The second barrier was related to the first. The completed surveys often listed fear of a mate's unknown response as the major reason why people did not engage in this type of prayer with their spouses, even though they desired it. In writing this book, we especially took into account that aspect of fear, specifically of not knowing the outcome if we make ourselves vulnerable to our mate. The risk involved in opening ourselves up to one another is that there is no guarantee that we will be accepted and loved for who we really are. We perceive a very real risk that we will be harmed, manipulated, judged deficient, or rejected. Just as physical intimacy requires vulnerability through being naked before one another, deep emotional and spiritual intimacy requires an even higher level of vulnerability.

Fear of one another is not innate. It is learned over the course of our lives, when even those we most love and trust inevitably hurt us. Fear is often generated from what is unknown—in this case, not knowing how to pray honestly and transparently with one's mate and not knowing how that mate will respond.

Therefore, we focused on two things to help break down the walls of fear and make the experience safer. First, we developed introductory materials and a set of exercises with lots of information and specific instructions to help decrease the unknown of how to pray intimately with your spouse without being a threat. Then we graduated the exercises to help decrease the potential fear associated with self-exposure so that the learning and experience curves would be gradual, allowing mutual trust to develop with practice and over time.

The third barrier was a lack of priority. Even though people specifically asked for materials to help them in their stated desire for this type of prayer—and even agreed to help us test the usefulness of the materials—not one of them had even begun to use the materials or move into this level of prayer on their own even a year later. Lack of priority was the single reason given for this outcome.

As we explored ways to enhance priority and follow-through for engaging in something that couples said they really wanted, we moved to a group format that would provide accountability and support for doing the prayer exercises. As opposed to the failed attempts of couples to complete the exercises on their own, this group stayed together for all twelve weeks of the pilot project. During that time, the couples faithfully completed the exercises and gave feedback each week about both the book content and their prayer experiences, to whatever degree they felt comfortable sharing with the group.

They all reported feeling safe during the exercises—even after initial trepidation when trying the more advanced ones—and said that they had engaged in rewarding and intimate prayer experiences, just as we had done when we'd practiced them in the process of developing the book. They also admitted that, without the accountability of the group, they would have had trouble maintaining the discipline of prioritizing their time to include this form of prayer, despite willing hearts. We strongly recommend utilizing a group—or at least one other couple—to take this journey with, and we have included suggestions in Appendix 3 for forming and participating in a couples prayer group using this book.

We owe a debt of gratitude to all of our friends who encouraged us to write a manual and who participated in the surveys—especially the first group to use these materials. They demonstrated to us that the book was worth the effort to write, worth the effort to use, and ultimately worth the effort to bring it to a larger audience.

We also owe much to the Presbyterian-Reformed Ministries International (PRMI) Dunamis Project, where we learned much about Holy Spirit-empowered prayer and the need to debrief spiritual experiences in order to discern whether or not what occurred was of God. We incorporated spiritual testing and debriefing into each exercise, modeled after the process taught and used in Dunamis courses.

God's revelation through the Holy Bible is the foundation for this book, which is strewn with Scripture references. (Our referencing and interpretation of them is taken from the King James Version.)

We owe all glory and honor to God alone and to His Holy Spirit for leading us to the truth of His words and for leading us on this journey so that we could pass it on to you.

Introduction

Our Invitation and Basic Information

We invite the two of you—Christians united in marriage, who both have a desire to develop spiritual intimacy with your mate through prayer with and for one another—to take the journey presented in this manual. Because it is in a workbook format with pages that need to be completed and notes that you may want to jot in the margins, each of you will need a copy.

It is possible for couples to use this book effectively on their own, if both individuals are very motivated and disciplined about their use of time without the need for outside accountability. However, we have not seen any couples, other than ourselves, follow through in using this book outside of a group where there is accountability and support. (See Appendix 3 for couples prayer group suggestions.)

The exercises themselves take about one to two uninterrupted hours per week, not counting preparation time. However, the times vary according to individuals and specific exercises. If you are participating in a group, factor in additional time to meet once per week for twelve weeks.

We hope that the experience of using this book of graduated prayer exercises will be so positive emotionally and spiritually that you and your spouse will want to continue this form of intimate prayer on your own.

Our Premise

We believe there is scriptural evidence to support our position that God, who created marriage, yearns for married couples to walk and talk with Him together, intimately relating to Him and each other. The garden of Eden in the book of Genesis is the place where God revealed His original plan for marriage, and it is the place to return to as the model of God's desire for couples.

The Song of Solomon is a picture of the intimacy and joy that God ordained for marriage between man and woman, as well as a picture of God's desire for intimacy and joy with us. In addition, 1 Corinthians 7:5 speaks of married couples abstaining from physical intimacy so that there can be a time for prayer. We believe that a married couple's prayer life can and should be as intimate as their physical relationship. It is even more vital to their marriage if God is to be the Lord of His creation. Intimate couple prayer, as presented in this book, is about coming together with your spouse in private to pray with and for each other, encountering your Creator as He participates with you, and growing in health and wholeness and holiness as a couple.

Matthew 18:20 is an invitation to join together with Jesus in prayer, the medium of intimacy that he knew best. Jesus did not need to experience the physical intimacy reserved by God for marriage in order to know the bounds of true intimacy. He risked complete vulnerability with his Father because he was secure in his relationship with Him. He sought time alone with his Father and established a communion so complete and deep that it would sustain him in Gethsemane, on the cross, and in hell itself.

Noticing this intimacy that Jesus had with his Father, Jesus' disciples asked him how to pray. He then gave them a format that could draw them into the same intimacy he shared with his heavenly Father, who was also their Father—and ours. This model prayer is our template for this book, broken down into exercises designed to take you and your spouse into deeper and deeper levels of prayer intimacy, with and for each other. The ultimate aim of the exercises is to take you on a journey back to the garden of Eden, where there are only the two of you and God, your Creator. In that place, through open and fearless three-way communion, you experience divine love poured out over you by your mate and by your doting Father God, just as Adam and Eve did before they broke off that communion through disobedience.

Your marriage and physical union entails a spiritual union (Malachi 2:15; 1 Corinthians 6:16b–17), and prayer is the way to take your spiritual union to the throne room of your Creator God to give and receive blessings that cannot be had any other way. Praying intimately with your mate builds up the emotional and spiritual bonds needed to establish, heal, and keep your marriage vital and strong.

From our experience, one of the greatest gifts that spouses can give each other is to come *together* to transparently pray. Together they place their needs and desires, joys and sorrows, triumphs and failures, strengths and weaknesses into the hands of Him who is able to do immeasurably more than we can think to ask or even imagine, simply because He loves us and our marriages more than we can ever ask or imagine (Ephesians 3:17–21).

Chapter 1

Purpose for the Journey: Spiritual Intimacy with Each Other and God

God was the original definer of intimacy in the book of Genesis. He created man and woman for physical, emotional, and spiritual intimacy, naked before and transparent with one another. He established His intimacy with Adam and Eve by walking and talking with them in His garden, where they were both naked before Him. He created them in an environment where fear of intimacy was not a concept, because they were abiding in His love, a place where fear could not dwell.

They began their journey living in perfect communion and harmony, united without the emotional and spiritual barriers of guilt, fear, and shame. However, they also began that journey with free will, and they were quickly put to the test of obeying their Creator. When Adam and Eve freely chose to obtain the knowledge of good and evil, they lost their innocence. Guilt, fear, and shame entered into their relationship with God and each other.

God did not run or hide from Adam and Eve, but they tried to hide from Him and from each other out of fear, erecting fig-leaf barriers to intimacy. God immediately called out to Adam and Eve at the point where they became afraid of Him, and He did not stop lovingly pursuing them and providing for them. From the moment that this innocence and intimacy was lost, God's whole theme throughout Scripture became one of continually reaching out, inviting the crown of His creation back into the intimate center of His holy, complete love. He made Himself safe to come near, through His mercy and grace, so that communion could be restored, and He gives us the choice of restoring intimacy with Him.

Because God was not willing to forsake communion with us, He gave us the means to make amends for our guilt through confession and forgiveness. He restored us so that we could put down our fig leaves and have an uninhibited and intimate relationship with Him and each other. Fearless and shameless nakedness means that we feel safe enough to bare our most private and deepest selves, not just physically but emotionally and spiritually. This may mean that most, if not all of us, have never experienced consistent intimacy with one another in marriage, because we have not found it consistently safe to reveal our innermost selves.

We hope that the readers of this book have a personal relationship with God, our heavenly Father, and that—imperfect as our human relationships may be for fostering intimacy—at least a trust base is already in place with God. Intimacy in prayer must first exist between each of us individually and God our Father. If we do not feel safe relating with God in our emotional and spiritual nakedness, knowing that He already sees us as we really are and loves us anyway, it may not be possible to arrive at deep levels of spiritual intimacy with another person.

On the other hand, even a deep and intimate relationship between God and the individual may not necessarily pave a smooth road for venturing into spiritual intimacy with our spouses. Sadly, it is all too common in marriages to find that it is easier to share our deepest selves with almost anyone but our spouses. It is all too common for deep and honest prayer to come more easily in almost any setting other than a private one with our spouses.

If God's intent for marriage was to establish it as the most intimate of all human relationships, how is it that physical intimacy can seem relatively easy while prayer intimacy seems so hard? How can we get back to God's garden, where we join with our mates, communing with God in His original design for intimacy with Him? Our hope is that this book will help with some of these tough issues and will set the stage for a return to the garden with your mate—to enjoy God and each other in the beauty of His holy presence, where it is safe to be naked and unashamed.

Preparation for the Journey

The journey cannot begin unless there is a desire on the part of both of you to grow together in prayer with and for each other. There must be a desire to build up one another emotionally and spiritually through prayer. You need to have a reasonably healthy relationship, where you relate to each other as equals with mutual respect and honesty, and where each of you trusts the other to act in your best interest. This section of the book contains some basic information on levels of emotional intimacy, personality dynamics, interpersonal communication, and differences between men and women, all of which impact emotional and spiritual intimacy and may be helpful in creating a better relationship—and ultimately a better prayer experience.

Taking Inventory: How Intimate Are You?

Emotional intimacy is a prerequisite for spiritual intimacy in marriage. If we briefly define intimacy as a close relationship built from an ongoing dialogue that allows each person to safely reveal their authentic selves, we have a framework for evaluating our relationships with both God and our spouse.

It may be helpful for you to evaluate the level of emotional intimacy you share with your spouse and to determine whether both of you desire to move to deeper levels. A simple model for evaluating emotional depth in relationships is presented below to assist you.

Emotional Depth-Finder

1. Level I: Surface exposed with very little self-disclosure, none to little trust needed, none to few risks taken
2. Level II: Below the surface but not total self-disclosure, moderate level of trust established, moderate risks taken
3. Level III: Deepest level of self-disclosure, total transparency, high level of trust established, high risks taken

Moving from the surface to deeper levels of intimacy requires the context of an appropriate relationship. Not all human relationships should move beyond the outward surface-level manifestations of moral, decent, Christlike behavior toward others, which neither require nor carry expectations of much self-disclosure.

Level I relationships are safe, in that they do not require much exposure of aspects of oneself that could result in rejection, invalidation, harsh judgment, condemnation, or shame, and there is not much investment in the relationship beyond cooperation in whatever situation both people are brought together in. The focus in this book is on Christian marriage, which is the ideal context for developing the deepest level of intimacy—physically, emotionally, and spiritually. The journey toward deep knowledge and acceptance of one another begins with a dialogue that moves two people beyond the safe surface of superficial knowledge toward deeper and truer revelations of self to one another.

As you take greater risks in revealing more of your true self, you hope that you will be received with acceptance rather than rejection and that your mate will reciprocate. Depending on both the desire to disclose and the response to each trial of disclosure, the journey toward intimacy either goes deeper, levels off, or moves back to a shallower level. If there is mutual desire to make oneself known and to affirm the other, rather than to withhold self and reject the other, more trust is built and more risk is taken, until, ideally, mutual transparency results.

Several things can undermine the move to a deeper level of emotional intimacy. One is a lack of reciprocity, where one person is moving toward increased self-disclosure, but the other is not, or at least not at the same rate. Sometimes one person holds back because he or she is not secure enough to show his or her true self. Other times, one holds back because he or she has no desire to become more emotionally intimate.

Another obstacle is the lack of a consistently affirming response when a person takes the risk of disclosure. Affirmation does not necessarily mean agreeing with what the person has disclosed. Rather, it means not judging or rejecting a person who reveals his true self and especially his human weaknesses. If there is a revelation by one party that cannot be affirmed by the other party because it is out of their bounds of acceptability, such as criminal behavior or infidelity, the relationship generally ends. Ideally, what we seek in a godly marriage is mutual affirmation as we make ourselves known to one another, even as we work individually and together toward Christlikeness.

All intimate relationships will invariably produce conflict. When love does not cover the relationship, conflict resolution cannot be love-based. When confession and forgiveness fail to heal and restore broken trust, a return to the safety of the surface at Level I often results. Even if the relationship survives, it may never return to the deeper levels that define true intimacy.

Until you have experienced the safety of an intimate relationship with God, you will not have a safe shelter to run to when human relationships disappoint and hurt, which is inevitable, given enough time and proximity. Only God can promise to always relate to you in love and can keep that promise, and Level III is often reserved for Him alone, rather than another person. As both of you strive to model Christ's love toward one another as he has loved you, you will be better equipped to go deeper than the surface of emotional and spiritual intimacy.

A marriage may exist at any of these three levels, but only levels two and three are intimate emotionally, regardless of sexual "intimacy." (And without emotional intimacy, it is more likely to be physical *union* rather than physical *intimacy*). Unless there is a mutual desire for deeper emotional intimacy, deeper spiritual intimacy between you and your spouse will not be possible, because the two are linked. It is possible to move deeper only when barriers are identified and removed. Fear is probably the biggest obstacle that inhibits a desire for self-revelation, and it can be overcome by a mutual commitment to build up one another in love.

If you and your spouse are not on the same level, it is possible that as a couple you can still grow deeper, both emotionally and spiritually, as long as you do not try to move deeper before both of you master the current level of emotional depth. Intimacy requires reciprocity. This means that there will be times when one spouse will need to share and hold, allowing the other spouse to catch up. Deep-sea diving together, like climbing together, ideally requires not going beyond each member's capacity or comfort level. Even if one or both of you is afraid to go deeper, there is something to be gained even in just going to the shallower levels of intimacy. As trust builds, deeper intimacy can be attempted.

On what level do you currently see your relationship? What are your reasons for your assessment? If you and your spouse do not agree with where you are, what do you see as the reasons for this discrepancy? If your desire is to go to a deeper level of intimacy emotionally and spiritually, what is blocking this in relationship to your mate? (The survey in Appendix 1 can be helpful here. If there are obstacles to praying together, they are probably the same as the blocks to greater emotional intimacy.) Discuss your answers to these questions with your spouse.

Jesus as Your Guide

Jesus modeled intimacy in his relationship to his followers, most notably his disciples and close friends. He started with an invitation to join him in relationship, responding to them at their level of understanding and spiritual growth. He would eventually come to call them his friends, even though they were far from perfect and far from being able to give back the same level of loyalty and commitment that he gave to them. Intimacy was possible because the disciples took the risk of living in tight community with Jesus, and because Jesus took the risk of relationship with them. He was in tight communion with his Father and did not depend on his disciples for his sense of identity and self-worth. He did not need the disciples in order to feel validated himself. His identity was with his Father, and he could afford the risk of intimate friendship with imperfect people because he was completely secure in his relationship with his Father.

The disciples trusted Jesus enough not only to follow and live with him but also to risk being honest and transparent with him. They did not always hide their weaknesses but instead brought them to light in their relationship with Jesus. Jesus was honest and transparent in return, keeping the relationship open by allowing the disciples to be who they were, without rejecting them based on who he was or what his expectations were. This did not mean that he did not have expectations in their relationship with him, but he never forced himself or his will on them or treated them with disrespect. They were always free to choose the depth of intimacy, and not all the disciples and friends had the same depth of relationship with Jesus.

The most notable in extremes are Judas Iscariot, who never got past himself and his own misguided agenda, and John or Peter, disciples that Jesus related to most intimately. His relationships with Martha, Mary, and Lazarus reflect close friendships that demonstrated mutual deep love, honesty, understanding, trust, and compassion.

His range of tolerance for the "slow learners" and "doubters" of the bunch was wide, as can be seen in Peter and Thomas. Rather than ridiculing them, he met them where they were in relationship to him, loving them enough to give them encouragement in ways that they personally needed, based on their particular personalities and human weaknesses. He communicated with his disciples at their levels of understanding, not ridiculing them when they failed to grasp his meaning. They felt free to ask him what he meant by some of the parables and some of his confusing statements and actions, and they were not inhibited or discouraged, even when he made it known that they should have grasped certain concepts. When they disappointed him, he responded from a heart of love.

Peter denied knowing him three times, but Jesus responded to the guilt-ridden man by seeking him out and restoring their relationship. Three times he asked his closest friends to stay awake and pray near him in the garden of Gethsemane on the worst night of his life. Although they failed him by falling asleep, he did not react with anger or abuse. Instead he turned to his Father alone and endured his pain and suffering without taking out his frustrations on those he called his friends.

The key to Jesus' relationships with his disciples and friends (which includes us, if we have chosen to live intimately with him), as well as with his Father, is a covenant of love—a binding agreement to a love that will nourish, sustain, build up, and not let go. A true love-covenant relationship is required before any deep level of intimacy can be achieved and maintained. The degree to which we are able to make and keep a love covenant with one another is the degree to which we will experience true intimacy with our mates.

Personality Differences

God is infinitely creative, and each of us carries His unique signature in how he created us, both physically and in personality. In our uniqueness, He gives each of us different aspects of Himself, which we do not always recognize as a gift from Him to one another. When we misunderstand differences and see them as deficits, we set the stage for failure in relationships. Just as misunderstanding God's character sets the stage for problems in our relationship with Him, so likewise do our misunderstandings of one another contribute to problems in our human relationships.

Some basic differences in our God-given personalities are easily grasped in the framework of the personality instrument known as the MBTI®, Myers-Briggs Type Indicator®. While this is a very brief overview, it may be helpful for the purposes of this book to spend some time on our fundamental differences, using this framework so that our differences do not create major obstacles in our relationship with God and each other, especially as related to prayer together.

According to the theory behind the MBTI, basic aspects of our personality are inborn, just as hand preference is. As such, there is not a "right or wrong" to your mind, any more than there is a "right or wrong" to being right- or left-handed. Obviously, "preference" does not mean that the *choices* you make in using your preferences are right or wrong: the preference in and of itself is neutral. But how or why you use that choice is right or wrong based on values and moral standards. Your personality preferences are never an excuse for un-Christlike behavior. All preferences were exhibited by Christ as our example of where, how, and when to use them.

The MBTI-based psychological model of personality describes four pairs of preferences for:

- The direction of mental focus and how you are energized (*extraversion* or *introversion*)
- How you take in information and what you pay attention to (*sensing* or *intuition*)
- How you come to conclusions and how you make decisions (*thinking* or *feeling*)
- How you live out your daily life and your attitude toward the external world (*judging* or *perceiving*)

A preference for *extraversion* is characterized by: mental attention focused outward, energy directed at and created by contact with others and the outer physical environment, talking things out in order to sort through one's thoughts, being easy to get to know, being sociable, having a broad range of interests, and being active and talkative.

A preference for *introversion* is characterized by: mental attention focused inward, energy directed at and created by being alone in order to focus and concentrate on concepts, ideas, and feelings, thinking through things in order to sort out one's thoughts, being harder to get to know, having intimate relationships that are few in number, having a smaller range of in-depth interests, and being reflective and quiet.

A preference for *sensing* is characterized by: taking in information through the five senses and paying attention to the specifics of the here and now, being reality-oriented through the physical senses, being practical and concrete, and focusing on specifics rather than the big picture.

A preference for *intuition* is characterized by: taking in information through hunches, inspiration, abstract ideas, and imagination, being possibility-focused and future-focused, and focusing on the big picture rather than the specifics.

A preference for *thinking* is characterized by: making decisions based on logical implications, objective principles, and truths, and being grounded in questioning and critiquing to form a firm analysis of the situation and a firm decision based on objectivity, regardless of the personal need or issue at hand.

A preference for *feeling* is characterized by: making decisions based on the impact on people, subjective values related to mercy and harmony, and being grounded in circumstances that may alter a decision, depending not on logical analysis but on the personal need or issue at hand.

A preference for *judging* is characterized by: the desire and ability to plan and organize one's outer world, coming to conclusions and fixing on a course of action without being dissuaded by never-ending possibilities and options.

A preference for *perceiving* is characterized by: the desire and ability to remain open to constant new options and possibilities in your outer world, and not fixing on a course of action until the last minute or until forced to by circumstances.

According to this theory-based model, you cannot use your mind for more than one mental function at a time: you are either taking in information or you are making conclusions or decisions about the information. There is a difference in how and when you use any of these functions, depending on your inborn preferences. All of us need to use all eight of the preferences at one time or another, even if they are not our own favorite or preferred functions. This is analogous to being forced to use your opposite hand if your dominant hand is broken, or having to use both hands because the situation calls for the use of more than one hand.

One obvious illustration related to type preference is for those of us who are *intuitives* by nature but who must also use *sensing* just to manage in our sensory world with tasks such as driving a car. The disadvantage to being in situations where you spend too much time having to use your non-favorite preference is that you will feel depleted of energy and even frustrated, as though you have to swim against the current. Try writing with your non-preferred hand for a day to experience the impact of being forced to be a "round peg in a square hole."

The advantage of being in a team with others who do not share your favorite preferences is that they can bring skill and energy to a relationship, providing the best of all possible ways to look at situations and come up with solutions. Unfortunately, without a framework that validates all personality preferences as gifts to one another, the usual result in relationships is a devaluing of those who do not see or interact with the world, or arrive at solutions, in the same way we do.

While this is a very brief explanation of the model for psychological differences, it will hopefully allow you to quickly see some attributes of yourself and others that are the same or different. Given that there are four scales with two polar-opposite functions for each, there are sixteen different combinations possible. While it is beyond the scope of this book to go into greater detail about each combination, it is possible to use this limited information to make some important points related to communication.

Extraverted types tend to "think out loud" when forming thoughts or opinions. Initial statements are rarely their final thought or position on a matter. Clarify with one another to find out if a thought is at its fullest development and final resting place. *Introverted* types are less comfortable sharing aloud either personal issues or thoughts that they have not had the quiet, uninterrupted time to finish processing before speaking them out. Clarify with one another to find out if more time and silent space is needed.

Sensing types concentrate on facts and realities in the practical here and now. *Intuitive* types tend to focus on possibilities with a future orientation. Clarify with one another to find out whether you are on the same wavelength in terms of what you are discussing and in what time frame—reality in the practical here-and-now or possibilities for the future.

Thinking types place high value on the process by which they have reached their conclusions, especially valuing logic, objectivity, and the truth of the situation. *Feeling* types place high value on the impact that any decision will have on the people involved, not on whether it is consistent with past or future decisions. Clarify with one another as to how you reached your decision, based on your orientation, and whether there needs to be further clarification in order to understand one another's position.

Judging types have a strong need to finalize decisions without leaving them up in the air until the last minute, including sticking with a plan or schedule. *Perceiving* types prefer to keep options open and often intentionally do not make decisions until the last minute. Given that new information may alter their position, they desire flexibility to accommodate late-coming information. Clarify with each other which issues are important enough to be settled or resolved now or in the near future, versus those that can be postponed.

Further pointers on communication, which incorporate type differences, are given in the next section.

Basics of Effective Interpersonal Communication

While the focus of this book is on prayer, it is three-way conversational prayer, and some basic pointers on effective communication are worth noting briefly. Use this as a checklist to assess strengths and areas needing improvement.

Prayer is conversation and communication *with* God, not talking *to* God. Likewise, couple prayer includes talking *with* your spouse, not *to* him or her. You can see the difference when you evaluate your words by the impact they have on communication. Do your words open or close the door to further dialogue? Too often, prayer sounds like a speech to God, where the one praying allows no room for response from God—or anyone else, if it is in the context of group prayer. The heart of communication is to be *connected*, one with another. Conversation is the exchange of thoughts, feelings, and ideas between individuals. Inherent in the art of communication is the ability to build connections between the participants.

Communication begins with effective listening. This is the hardest part of communication, because it requires giving full attention to the speaker. It involves hearing the feelings and meanings in the words, and being able to respond in a way that demonstrates that understanding has occurred. It requires being able to reflect back what you've heard in an effort to clarify whether you truly understood the speaker. This is not possible if your mind is formulating a response while the speaker is talking. Listening and formulating thoughts of your own are mutually exclusive and separate activities, which is where most communication breaks down.

Talking *to* someone is one-sided. It is characterized by pronouncements, commands, or lack of permission and space for the listener to ask for clarification, to respond, or to *interact* with the speaker. In conversation—where the purpose is dialogue—the speaker may shut down the process of talking *with* by going on at such length or complexity that the listener gets lost.

Talking *with* invites participation from the listener. It is characterized by the role-sharing that occurs when participants alternately listen and speak. It gives permission and space for the listener to clarify the speaker's statements when needed, and it invites responses from the listener.

Communication means owning your own thoughts, feelings, and behaviors, and not speaking for others. Speaking for others is especially common in group prayer, where a speaker says something like, "Lord, we really feel blessed by you." The reality may very well be that there are those present—and included in the "we"—who do not really feel blessed by the Lord at that moment.

While this may not present serious problems in some settings, in couple prayer it undermines the recognition that there are two separate people who need a framework for being open and honest, if true intimacy is to be experienced. This requires being free and able to speak for oneself, owning one's own thoughts, feelings, and, especially, behaviors. Most messages that show where the ownership lies are identified with the word *I* as opposed to *you* or *we*. Messages that start with *you* or *we* may result in the other person feeling labeled, blamed, misrepresented, and ultimately misunderstood.

Respect-based communication means honoring the other person by using words that are love-based, including speaking truth bound with mercy, and by listening with full attention and openness. This means that there is no room in conversation for sarcasm, ridicule, pressure, or any demeaning speech. When we are truly listening, there is no room for judging the message or preparing a comeback. Listening with full attention means waiting for all of the message to be given before responding—and even repeating it to yourself before responding to the other person. It sometimes means asking clarifying questions to make sure you have heard correctly before assuming the message has been received as intended.

Basic courtesies include not interrupting one another and not filling up silence with talking. Just as silence may be needed for a response to be formulated by the listener, God needs our silence. Breaking that silence before God has either started or finished speaking undermines His presence in the three-way conversation of couple prayer. Obviously, on the human level we need to work out a system of communication and understanding that will help us not to interrupt a silence needed by our spouse, ourselves, and God. Hand signals can be very effective, as long as both of you know and agree upon the meaning and they are value-neutral. Jan makes it a point to pray with her eyes open when praying with others, because facial expressions often give indications of what others need.

Remember that personality type preferences are present in communication. Refer to the previous section as needed, and when there appears to be a glitch in communication, use the framework of personality type to sort out and solve the problem. This will keep the focus on constructive use of differences rather than destructive attacks on differences between you and your spouse.

When we communicate with each other, our interaction should match the reverence with which we speak and listen to God. Too often we revere and honor God in prayer (at least publicly), only to treat others with disrespect. The book of James speaks specifically to this issue in James 3:9–11. We use our tongues to praise God, and then we put down other people, who are created in God's image.

Conflict Resolution Script

It is inevitable that two people will clash at times because of competing desires. Usually in conversation (prayer included), the competing need is to speak and ask questions at the same time the other person wants to speak. Sometimes the need is to engage the other party in conversation when the other party does not wish to be engaged—either because he or she needs time and silence to formulate a response, or because he or she does not want to dialogue—and conversation requires some level of engagement by *both* parties. The following "script" is offered as a template to help clarify the problem and focus on solutions. Complete these partial statements.

- "*I have a problem with ...*" (This must be a specific, observable behavior, without the other person attached to it.)
- "*I feel ...*" (This must be a personal feeling, not an accusatory "that you" statement or an "I think" statement that dodges expressing an emotion.) *because ...* (This must name a specific behavior of the other person.)
- "*I would like ...*" (This must be a concrete behavior that is realistic and constructive to the problem at hand.)

An example of this, using a problem that occurs frequently, can be stated as follows: "I have a problem with being interrupted before I am finished with what I have to say. I feel devalued and hurt because you interrupt me before I am finished with my thought. I would like to try using a tennis ball so that we will know when one of us is finished so that the other person can speak. If one of us is holding the ball, we will release it when we are done. That way, you will know when I am finished speaking." Now the ball (literally or figuratively) is in the other person's court for offering a response to try this approach, modify it, or suggest something else. If one solution does not work, keep trying to modify or change the solution options until the problem is resolved without undermining the relationship or "throwing in the towel" on communication or prayer together.

In our case, personality type dynamics cause this situation to come up all the time. Wayne is introverted in preference, needing space, silence, and time to work out in his head what he is thinking before he speaks. Jan, on the other hand, is extraverted in preference. She does her thinking by talking out loud in order to clarify her thoughts and then arrive at a final thought. Interruptions are not interpreted as negative to her because they add to her thought process. If Wayne is talking in depth and at length, Jan gets lost without some ability to clarify or respond after one or two sentences. However, if Jan interrupts Wayne's carefully constructed thought before it is spoken in its entirety, he has difficulty picking up where he left off in order to respond to a question or thought interjected by Jan.

Dialogue does not mean the same thing to us in terms of our individual personality preferences, and we have to continuously work out our differences. We deal with this by clarifying up front whether the person speaking wants to converse (where dialogue dynamics need to be considered), or whether one of us just needs to "think out loud" or vent. If there is a thought process going on where the need is to put thoughts out on the table for consideration later, Jan frequently takes notes. She also takes notes during prayer and at other times when interruption would not be appropriate or could cause the person praying to lose track of where the Holy Spirit is leading.

Gender Differences

One of the biggest areas of struggle for true intimacy is the God-created differences between men and women. Not only do these differences affect our physical, mental, and emotional natures, but they profoundly affect how men and women relate to God. In the earlier section on personality differences, the focus was on differences that are not gender-specific. While it is essential to understand personality preferences that impact communication in order to both appreciate and understand those who are not our personality type, it is also essential to understand some basic and very real gender-specific dynamics that are present, regardless of personality preferences.

There are many studies and books that contribute to our understanding of biological and innate differences in gender, but the Bible, if read in context and without cultural filters, provides a comprehensive view that is in total agreement with the best that modern science and secular studies have to offer. God is the author of all truth, so it should not be surprising that true science, which is invested in discovering truth, matches God's own book on the subject.

Originally, in the garden of Eden, God created man and woman both in His own image, and although they were biologically, mentally, emotionally, and spiritually different, they were both, equally, at the pinnacle of God's creation. Neither sex was exalted above the other, even though they were not identical. They were to be companions and helpmates to one another, using their own unique aspects of their gender to compliment one another as co-tenders of God's garden. Their fellowship with God and one another was without any inhibitions or barriers.

However, God had created them with free will so that their love of Him and one another would be a free choice. Regarding one specific tree in the garden, God told them to not eat fruit from it, and He gave them the consequences for disobedience. Both of them were given the choice of obedience and a life of free and open relationship with their Creator God and one another. They both chose disobedience, leading to the loss of their free and open relationship with their Creator and with each other. *The way* they chose disobedience reveals differences between men and women, and once God removed them from the garden, He magnified the differences between them.

God created us with obvious physical differences, magnified after God sent Adam and Eve from the garden. Women are physically constructed for childbearing, and men are physically constructed for brute strength. Because we are body, mind, and spirit, all facets of body affect mind and spirit. Our minds produce the thoughts that produce the feelings and emotions that lead to our actions. Our thoughts, feelings, and actions influence and are influenced by both body and spirit.

We laugh at (or wince at, if we are honest with ourselves) caricatures such as the manipulative "innocent and helpless female" who seduces men like a black widow spider, or the "cave man" who uses a club to subdue both wild beasts and women. There is some truth hidden in both examples, given that the extreme misuse of the way God created us leads to these negative stereotypical images. If men and women are indeed to glorify God, they must come to terms with how God created them by recognizing that God chose to create both male and female in His image. It is through our very differences that God's image is most completely reflected, especially in marriage.

After the original split between the first couple and God, He spent the entire remainder of the Bible revealing His heart in order to draw us back to Himself, to a relationship where harmony and true intimacy is restored. The only way back to fellowship in God's garden is through admitting that we are born rebellious, which varies in its manifestations by both personality type and gender. Going back to the garden requires going to our Creator God, repenting of our rebellion, and receiving forgiveness—ultimately through the atoning death of Jesus.

With confession, however, we only get to the garden gate. Unless there is true repentance, which means both owning and turning away from our rebellious behavior, barriers remain in our intimacy with God and one another. The fig leaves, or barriers, between men and women as well as God, appear as gender-based patterns. This can be seen throughout the Bible in the behaviors, attitudes, and choices made—good and bad—by both men and women.

Men's Issues versus Women's Issues: Expectations That
Set the Stage for Miscommunication

- Men identify more readily with physical power and action for the purpose of achieving solutions to concrete and tangible problems. Women identify more readily with emotional affiliation and attachment to others for the purpose of achieving relationships that are intimacy-oriented.

- Men identify with ethics of rights and justice, which may mean using violence as a means of achieving what is perceived as right and just. Women identify with ethics of care and responsibility to others, which are prefaced by doing no harm and, ideally, preventing harm.

All of these gender differences are legitimate and necessary for a fully functioning society, and they are best captured in God's own words. In answer to the question of what He requires of His people, He states that we are to *do* what is just, *be* merciful, and *walk* with Him in humility (Micah 6:8). Doing justice appears to fit a man's nature, while being merciful appears to fit a woman's nature. But *both* are required to ensure that *both* justice and mercy are manifested, and *both* man and woman are required to walk humbly with God.

Men's Issues That Can Undermine Unity

Adam's original sin occurred within his relationship with Eve and the beginnings of the first family, and the first sin between siblings occurred shortly thereafter. History has been a continuing saga of rebellion from the very beginning—to the degree that what seems "right" and "just" and "loving" is so perverted that God's requirements of us bear no resemblance to His original intent when He created us to be in unity with Him. We are blind to the land mines that Satan, the Father of Lies, has strewn about our landscape, because we are constantly looking through dark glasses that are created by our own flesh and imperfect humanity rather than through spiritual eyes that are created by God to help us correct and heal our distorted images of ourselves, others, and God Himself.

Because God clearly gave the responsibility to husbands to be a covering of protection over their spouses and children (1 Peter 3:7), husbands are in a very precarious place with God if they fail to meet His expectations of them. Men will be judged more harshly, just as God judged Adam more harshly—even though Eve committed the first act of rebellion and he followed. He watched as she fell for the Serpent's lies and did nothing to correct the lies or stop the results (Genesis 3:6).

To raise ourselves and our marriages to the level of health and abundance that God intends for us to have, husbands must seek out and acknowledge their shortcomings as husbands and spiritual heads of their households. This means yielding themselves to Jesus' undistorted character, which is the truth, the life, and the way of God's love (John 14:6). Husbands who are bound by lies regarding their masculinity and roles as husbands cannot love their wives at all. The extent to which our definitions of truth and love and life do not match up with Jesus is the extent to which husbands do not love their wives—or even themselves. If they have not conformed to the character of Christ as new creations in Christ, their self-love is distorted, and the command to love their wives as they love themselves (Ephesians 5:28–29) results in a perversion of God's gift of marriage.

Following are some of the land mines for men that need to be located and deactivated in the marriage landscape to avoid undermining unity between spouses.

- Distorted thinking regarding "submission" leads to the lie that women must be subjugated to men, especially their husbands, regardless of whether the husband is submitted to God or the spouses are submitted to each other (Ephesians 5:21–33) Husbands often misuse submission to control and bully, rather than operate out of love for the benefit of their wives. God never tries to control others; He draws people to him with love, and they choose to yield their lives to him and give him authority over them.

- Distorted thinking regarding hierarchy leads to the lie that men and women are not equals. God created both male and female to reflect His image, with neither exalted above the other (Genesis 1:27). If we are in relationship with Jesus, there is no hierarchy, neither male nor female (Galatians 3:28). Where hierarchy is spelled out (Ephesians 5:22–33), it is preceded by twenty-one verses about how we should imitate God and walk in His love.

- Distorted thinking regarding men relating physically and mentally but not emotionally leads to the lie that men must not feel or express emotions that reflect the more "feminine" side of how God created us. Look at the range of emotions expressed by Jesus, including weeping in front of his close friends. Anger is the one emotion that men are taught to express easily, and unless it is expressed in a Christlike way, it is sin. Too often, anger is used to intimidate and shut down communication with women. At the very least, this is a form of control and manipulation and can lead to emotional and physical abuse.

- Distorted thinking that women are "emotional" and not capable of physical and mental competence leads to the lie that their thoughts and actions should be ignored by men. God created us all with physical, mental/emotional, and spiritual attributes, and we are commanded to love God with all of these three aspects of the way He created us (Deuteronomy 6:5).

- Distorted thinking regarding communication leads to the lie that actions are enough to demonstrate caring, regardless of attitude and without engaging in dialogue. Throughout Scripture, Jesus was seen repeatedly relating to men, women, and children on whatever level his love could best be communicated to them—based on their need, not his.

- Distorted thinking that women are the "spiritual" ones leads to the idea that men don't have to develop this part of their nature. Adam's sin was in this exact area: He left his relationship with God up to Eve, even though he was to be her partner, and he even blamed his sin on her. It is interesting to note that part of the penalty assigned to her was to place her husband over her in hierarchy, where none existed before. Husbands need to take responsibility for their own spiritual development, because they are the spiritual, as well as physical, heads of their households, and they will be judged according to the degree that their headship is Christlike.

Women's Issues That Can Undermine Unity

Women, being created in God's image with the same value to God as men, need to reconcile themselves to having attributes of their Creator God that are different from men's. One of the biggest pitfalls in marriage relationships is the expectation that our opposite-sex spouse views, values, and reacts to life from the same place we do. Given the difficulty of placing ourselves in the shoes of others so that we can communicate and love each other more appropriately and completely, it is no wonder that Paul refers to both marriage and the church as a mystery.

Physically created to contain, birth, and nurture life, women relate to the world, others, and God through the lens of personal human connections that may either totally confuse their spouses or put unfair expectations on them. Just as there are land mines in the marriage landscape that need to be located and deactivated by men, women need to do likewise, given that their rebellion and human blindness need to be brought into the presence of the one true Light so that they can be healed and made whole, not just for their own sakes, but for those they care for and about. They cannot have authentic, intimate relationships with their spouses or God, if they have preconceived notions about either of them.

Following are some of the land mines for women that are common in the marriage landscape and can undermine unity with their spouses.

- Distorted thinking that women are coequals in creation so that there is no basis for submission leads to the lie that submission is a form of bondage and not the route to freedom through submission to Jesus Christ. This land mine can only be deactivated where the husband has dealt with his own distortions in this area, as no mentally or spiritually healthy woman would willingly and joyfully submit to an abusive husband.

- Distorted thinking of the opposite Scripture—that women are the weaker vessels— leads to the lie that, as the weaker ones, women do not need to take responsibility to live a life obedient to God, because their husband is their covering. We are all called individually to take full responsibility for our own sin (Ezekiel 33:20b), and nowhere does Scripture teach that we are to obey our husbands *over* God.

   Numerous examples throughout Scripture show that we are called to do what is right in the sight of God—a higher calling than all others. This means that we are to be active agents in refusing to do evil. Moses was delivered from death by midwives who feared God more than those in authority over them, and Rahab lied to save those whom she knew worshipped the one true God.

   In Scripture, submitting to any authority presumes that the authority is not in direct conflict with the commands, will, and character of God, whom we are to fear more than man. Matthew 10, especially verse 28, talks about the cost of discipleship, and

Jesus states in verses 34 and 35 that his sword will divide even families and will not bring peace, unless those under the same roof are submitted to Christ and love him first and foremost.

- Distorted thinking that women are not allowed to feel or express the full range of emotions that God created them with leads to the lie that the more "masculine" emotion of anger and the passionate expression of outrage are not permissible. This lie leads women *not* to speak truth in the image of Christ, which is a sin of omission rather than commission. God clearly states throughout His Word that we are to love what He loves and hate what He hates. The ultimate issue is whether, in expressing ourselves, we are not crossing over into sin in our thoughts and actions.

- Distorted thinking that women are entitled to be "emotional" and "irrational" leads to the lie that emotions are an acceptable excuse to avoid responsibilities and true communication. A somewhat stereotyped example is the presence of tears: those that are genuine are not sin, but tears used to gain sympathy or to avoid issues are sin. Manipulation of another person's emotions through how you express your own emotions is emotional blackmail. It is a game that either sex can play, and it is sin and an abomination to God.

- Distorted thinking that women are more spiritually minded potentially leads to minimizing their husband's spiritual expressions or to becoming spiritually conceited. In 1 Peter 3:1–4, Peter speaks of winning over our spouses who may not be obedient to God through our godly behavior rather than words, treating our spouses with respectful and pure conduct, and focusing on the inner beauty of a gentle and quiet spirit, which is precious to God.

Gender Differences in How We Relate to God and His Son, Jesus

The prayer that Jesus taught the disciples progresses to deeper levels of intimacy with God. Moving to deeper levels of spiritual intimacy with our spouses, using this prayer as a model, needs to take into account gender differences. While both sexes can relate to God as our heavenly Father, our Creator, our provider, our Great Physician, etc., God gave us a perfect human in order to more fully experience His nature and His plan of redemption for all of creation. An intimate relationship with the man Jesus draws us into greater intimacy with God.

However, relating to Jesus can be confusing, depending on which male attributes we are focused on. There is probably no other area that so confuses intimacy with Jesus for men than biblical references to the church as the bride and Jesus as the bridegroom. Women can relate to being his bride, because he is male in human form, and being his bride means having the protective covering of his love (Song of Solomon 2:4). While this is a picture of both headship and intimacy, men simply cannot relate to themselves as a bride and Jesus as their husband.

There are many references to Jesus that men can much more readily identify with, such as *Lord, kinsman, shepherd, redeemer, teacher,* and even *friend.* Jesus is in a very masculine role as commander of the Lord's army (Joshua 5:15) and in his second coming, *not* as a baby or a lamb but on a white horse as a warrior and king (Revelation 19:11–16). We cannot come into any level of intimacy with Jesus without first seeing him as someone desirable to be with and worthy of being called our Lord, just as the disciples and his other followers did. We get to that point in different ways that are influenced by many things, including personality, circumstances, and gender differences.

Intimacy with Jesus came about with his first followers, because they initially saw value in his invitation to a relationship, which they built by becoming his disciples and living in community with him. In the book of John, the most intimate portrait of Jesus and his relationships with others, Jesus came to the final days of his earthly life and taught his disciples about the greatest love, which is to lay down one's life for a friend. He then told his disciples that they were no longer just servants to him but his friends (John 15:12–17).

Both men and women should be able to relate to this model view of marriage. It is an intimate, servanthood-based friendship with our mate, which comes from knowing that our best interests and our life itself is foremost to our spouse.

Chapter 2

Process for the Journey:
The Lord's Prayer for Couples

It is no accident that the Lord's Prayer is a common denominator for all Christians and is the best known of all Christian prayers. Given that Jesus was asked by his disciples how to pray, it is really a misnomer to call it the *Lord's* prayer. In reality it is the model prayer for all disciples, as given by Jesus, who, more than any other person, had absolute and perfect intimacy with His Father through prayer. If this prayer can be seen as the model for spiritual intimacy, then it makes sense to use it as our model for spiritual intimacy as a married couple.

The following is our modified variation of Matthew 6:9–13.

Our Father in heaven,
Holy is your name.
May your kingdom come, and
May your will be done here on earth, as it already is in heaven.
Give us today all that we need.
Forgive us the wrongs we have done,
As we forgive the wrongs that others have done to us.
Protect us from hard testing,
And free us from the influence of the Evil One.
Your kingdom, your power, and your glory belong to you forever.
Amen.

The Lord's Prayer

"Our Father"

Our very first experience with intimacy in relationships is between parent and child. In a healthy parent-child relationship, the child is free to fully trust and expect that all his needs will be met with love. In the parent-child relationship—where trust is established through faithfulness on the part of the parent, with no expectations or conditions placed on the child— the child is free to take the relationship for granted. That is, it's a guaranteed relationship, no matter what.

If this base of trust is not established adequately in our first intimate relationship with our parent(s), we will continue to struggle with insecurity and lack of trust in other intimate human relationships—most specifically, marriage. Our Father wants us to go to Him as our safe refuge, never outgrowing our need for Him, and growing even more in need of Him as we risk the most intimate of human adult relationships: marriage.

"In Heaven"

Because no earthly parent can demonstrate perfect love to his child, Jesus makes the distinction that his Father is the perfect one in His perfect domain, heaven. This is important for all of us to know, but it is especially important for those of us who had less-than-adequate parents on earth. Until we gain a corrective experience through our relationship with our Father in heaven, we will be unable to take His love as "guaranteed." We need this corrective relationship before we can take the risk of loving and being loved by another imperfect human.

Through this corrective and perfect love relationship with God, we can withstand our own imperfections, as well as our mate's, and go to Him for lessons on loving ourselves and each other more perfectly. We will all struggle with our relationship to God, not knowing how to receive or respond to His perfect love completely, until we are finally made perfect in heaven. But His love is not less available to us now. To the extent that we consciously put away our limiting comparisons of God to our earthly parents, we will receive His corrective love relationship now, in this lifetime.

"Holy Is Your Name"

A name assigned to something describes its character. Likewise, the name of God describes His character. The word *holy* comes from derivations of *hallowed* in Old English and means "whole, wholesome, heal, or healed." God's character, as implied by a name that means whole and healed, is perfect good, or perfect love. God is set apart from His creation by His perfection, but He is fully trustworthy and can be taken as "guaranteed" by His very perfection.

"Your Kingdom Come"

God is King over all creation, and His kingdom in heaven is fully realized, with perfect submission to His rule and reign. While it is true that there is still a battle raging in the heavens (Ephesians 6:12), this is not to be confused with the heaven where Jesus is seated far above all forces of evil (Ephesians 1:16–23). Satan, our enemy, must still ask permission of God to act against those of us who belong to Him (Job 1:6–12).

As our two lives come together in intimacy under His rule and reign, all His goodness comes to earth in our marriage, in spite of the battle raging against us. He has given us Himself, and we must appropriate Him as our protection (Ephesians 6:10–20). We are likewise equipped by God for every good work, which is the manifestation of His kingdom on earth (2 Corinthians 9:6–15). God chose marriage on earth to be the very model and mystery of the church as the bride of Jesus Christ, the bridegroom.

"Your Will Be Done"

God's desire is that we experience the perfect goodness of His character on this earth during this lifetime, but it depends on our submission to His rule and reign in our lives individually. He cannot give us what we refuse to come into His kingdom to receive. God cannot contradict His nature, which is perfect good, perfect love. He is the safest king we could ever submit our allegiance to. He is the only king worthy of our total submission, because he is the only king who can guarantee perfect love toward us in response to our submission to His authority.

As our two lives come into perfect unity through submission to the will of our Father, He is able to grant us all that He has for us in His kingdom here on earth.

"Give Us Today All That We Need"

Just as a child who is secure in a trusting bond with a loving parent does not even consider or worry whether or not he will have all his needs met, we likewise can trust that our Father will provide daily, day after day, all that we need. Just as a loving parent longs to have his child connect to him in dialogue, so our heavenly Father longs to have dialogue with us.

All we have to do is *ask*, and the dialogue begins. His perfect love casts out all fear of being left in need by our imperfect mates, who—no matter how close to Christlikeness they become in this lifetime—will never be able to meet all our daily needs, every day, forever.

"Forgive Us The Wrongs We Have Done To One Another, Just As
We Forgive One Another The Wrongs Done To Us."

Just as a good and loving parent will not leave his child as an infant by protecting him from realities that produce growth, neither will our heavenly Father. Having built His trust base for us by faithfully meeting all our needs, He is now exposing us to realities that will challenge us to grow, both toward Him and toward one another. He has established Himself as safe to submit to, and now He gives us both reality and challenge under His authority.

God knows that we cannot keep ourselves from the self-centered desire to rule over our own lives and be subject to no one. So, given the reality of our selfish nature, He challenges us to acknowledge our selfishness that causes harm to others, especially those we are most intimate with. Then He gives us freedom from our guilty selfishness through His forgiveness when we ask. But He stretches us beyond ourselves by linking our freedom to forgiving those who have hurt us. He has now moved us out of deeper intimacy with Him alone to deeper intimacy with our beloved, through our asking, giving and receiving forgiveness from one another.

"Protect Us from Hard Testing"

An earthly parent has to keep pace with the developing child's growing sense of freedom and autonomy, giving enough freedom for growth, but not so much that the child would be in danger of great harm. So also our heavenly Father desires that we learn that freedom has necessary limits to keep us from great harm. He tests us by allowing us to enter into tempting situations, so we will learn by our mistakes that His ways are best for us.

He also tests us with situations that increase our trust and reliance on Him when the situation looks hopeless. Knowing that we can ask anything of our Father, we are encouraged to ask for His constraints that would keep us from harm through temptations that are too hard for us to resist and tests that are too hard to endure. This is especially important, because anything that affects us also affects our beloved mate, given that intimacy creates the bonds that do not allow for one to be harmed without also harming the other.

"Free Us from the Influence of the Evil One"

Just as we fail to heed the limits placed upon us by our earthly parents when we do not heed their wisdom, so we fail to heed the limits and boundaries placed upon us by our heavenly Father. While God is faithful to not give us challenges and life tests that are too hard to master, we, in our childish arrogance, think we are wiser, refusing to resist or take the ways of escape He provides when we stray from His path for us.

Just as a child whose parent has forged a strong bond of trust can call on that parent in times of trouble and expect a loving response and even rescue, we can call on our heavenly Father to rescue us and free us from the influence of the Enemy. We will inevitably fail in some of our testings, when resisting temptation seems impossible. When we succumb, we need Him to restore us through our repentance and His forgiveness.

Next, we need God to free us from the Evil One's influence so that we will be able to walk with Him, not losing sight of the righteous path He has set us on. We all have "prodigal son" experiences, and at the point where we humbly turn our hearts back to our Father, He will welcome us with open arms, running to us and bringing us into His fortress of love. In that place, the Evil One cannot enter. If our mate is there as well, we are reunited in holiness, not only with our Father but in our marriage, which is sacred. Our goal should be to stay in that place, free from the temptation to ever leave it.

"Your Kingdom, Power And Glory Belong To You Forever."

With no expectations of such, the parent who has wisely raised his child may be blessed enough to hear his child's affirmation of his wisdom. The parent may live long enough to hear the grateful child acknowledge that the parent did indeed love him, and he may even be fortunate enough to hear his child sing his praises.

At last, in this prayer, our heavenly Father receives His affirmation. We have come together in a sacred assembly of marriage to worship and glorify Him who gives only what is good and perfect for us, our Father, who never changes his position toward us and who is the light that drives out all darkness of evil (James 1:17).

"Amen"

So be it. The parent and child are in deep agreement about the truth of their relationship.

We are one with the Father through his Son, Jesus, and by his Holy Spirit, we are in deep agreement about the truths of our relationship through oneness in marriage. God our Father has given us as gifts to each other, and as believers together, we are in the role of the bride, united with Christ as our bridegroom and head of our marriage.

Levels of Prayer Intimacy for Couples

Using the Lord's Prayer as a model, each level described below is designed to move couples from safe surface levels to more intimate and penetrating levels that require more exposure, vulnerability, and risk with each other. Through a process of systematically moving through each level, spouses will have the opportunity to experience a deeper communion with each other and with God.

Level 1: "Our Father, Holy is your name."
- Praise, thanksgiving, and acknowledgment of God to God

Level 2: "Your kingdom come, your will be done."
- Praise, thanksgiving, and acknowledgment of each other as God's gift to each other
- Blessing each other according to God's will
- Submission to Jesus Christ as head of your marriage

Level 3: "Give us this day."
- Petitions for felt needs: physical, mental/emotional, and spiritual

Level 4: "Forgive us, protect us, deliver us."
- Confession and forgiveness of self and each other
- Protection: praying protection for each other
- Deliverance: praying freedom for each other

Level 5: "Your kingdom, power, and glory are yours. Amen."
- Deep worship of God
- Deep agreement with Christ

Introduction to Prayer Exercises for Couples

The series of exercises that follow in chapter 3 are modeled on the Lord's Prayer. They begin with straightforward praise and proceed gradually to deeper levels.

The sequence of the exercises is very important, and they should initially be completed in order. It is okay to repeat an exercise that you have already completed, especially if one or both of you is not comfortable moving to the next exercise after first reading it.

All exercises assume that there is mutual agreement to pray together. They also assume your agreement as to the level of prayer that is comfortable for both of you.

The exercises do not assume any prior experience in praying together, so we have tried to keep the steps simple and basic.

Even if you do pray together regularly, the exercises may provide a means of renewing the vitality and depth of your prayer life.

Framework for Prayer Time

1. *Freedom from distractions*: Schedule a time to pray when you will be free from known interruptions. Both of you need to commitment to this time. Otherwise, it is too easy to let the busyness of everyday life steal away your good intentions.

2. *Phone interruptions*: Decide ahead of time whether or not you will answer the phone if it rings. If you decide not to answer it, it may help to shut the volume off or unplug it so it won't be distracting. If you do decide to allow interruptions, be prepared for the reality that momentum and intimacy will be lost.

3. *Time limit*: If you have not prayed together before, or pray together very seldom, you might want to set a time limit that is mutually agreeable. This time limit should be one that is acceptable to (and even suggested by) the party that is least comfortable with the exercise. Honesty regarding the time limit is important. Because you are meeting the Lord in prayer *together*, you need to meet Him in a time frame that both of you can manage comfortably. If one partner desires a longer time, consider that patience and joining with your spouse is more important at this stage than your own felt needs.

   If you have not prayed together before, fifteen minutes may be a good limit with which to start. Set a limit that is comfortable for both of you, but don't feel that you need to make the preset limit a mandatory cutoff point. It may be that the Holy Spirit takes you into a new level of awareness of the presence of God. If so, check with each other to see if you both desire to continue past your time limit. Take advantage of such opportunities when you can; they may be times when the Lord wants to do something special with one or both of you.

4. *Frequency*: As a rule of thumb, once a week is probably the minimum. If you are praying together for the first time, you need to maintain some continuity in your practice of prayer. Otherwise, it will be more difficult to build on your experience. Prayer should not be forced, but neither should it be approached as "catch as catch can." The Enemy does not

want you praying together and will send all kinds of distractions and reasons why you can't do it this week. So do the best you can, but don't feel like failures (another favorite accusation of the Enemy) if you miss a week every now and then.

5. *Posture or position*: Find a comfortable position in which to pray. Feel free to vary this as needed, and don't feel constrained by preconceived notions of how prayer *should* be done. For example, it is not possible to read Scripture with your eyes closed, so do not feel that prayer can only happen if you have your eyes shut or your head bowed. However, if you want to express an attitude of reverence by those actions, then by all means do so.

In praying together, you are entering into a place of spiritual closeness with each other and with your heavenly Father. If it feels appropriate for your physical posture to reflect your spiritual posture, then sit together in a way that does so. Hold hands if you feel like it, but do not feel like you are failing to be truly spiritual if you don't feel like it. Just do what is comfortable for both of you, focus on the awesome God who made you and loves you, and don't worry about how you compare to anyone else in your prayer time with Him.

6. *Permission to stop*: You or your spouse may need to stop an exercise before it is finished due to loss of emotional comfort resulting from fear, conflict, feeling manipulated, etc. If this happens, try to share with your spouse your reason for stopping. Use the Conflict Resolution Script on pages 11-12, and schedule another time to try the exercise again.

Guidelines for Praying Together

1. *Praying out loud*: If you are not comfortable praying out loud in a group, remember that this time only your spouse and the Lord Himself will be listening. If you have gotten this far, you can be assured that neither of them will be sitting in judgment of how eloquent or spiritual you are. They both simply want to hear from you about what is on your heart so that the three of you can be real with each other.

2. *Praying single thoughts*: If you are praying together for the first time, or praying out loud for the first time, it may be easier to start with single sentences or single-thought prayers. In this style of prayer, you just pray a single thought as simply as possible, without feeling pressured to explain or elaborate on your thought. You do not literally have to limit yourself to just a single sentence, but focusing on a single thought or point without elaborating is important to allow for your spouse to pray in response.

Lengthy prayer covering a variety of thoughts and subjects is not conducive to conversational prayer. In couple or group prayer, it is as inhibiting as a general conversation that doesn't stay on the subject at hand or allow the other parties to respond. Each exercise in this book provides the topic and steps so that your prayer time stays focused.

3. *Praying conversationally*: There are three of you present, and what you are doing is like a conversation in which each person contributes his or her thoughts and ideas, focusing on a specific topic. To facilitate this, the exercises contain specific instructions for taking turns with single thoughts. In addition, allow some silent space in the conversation for responses from your spouse, and especially from the Holy Spirit. In doing so, be open to thoughts along the same prayer theme that the Holy Spirit will give to you during the spaces of silence, and pray those out loud if they seem to fit.

4. *Using words of Scripture in prayer*: If you have not prayed using Scripture before, it is worthwhile at this point to practice putting Scripture into your own words and converting the content into prayer form. We used lots of Scripture in this book, and we put it into our own words instead of quoting from a Bible translation, because it was important to us that we really understood the meaning in context and application. Examples of this are included in the first six exercises.

    Advance preparation gives you the time to locate relevant Scriptures. Feel free during your prayer time to search the Bible for verses that the Holy Spirit may be leading you to pray, but it is best not to take up too much time searching for verses you cannot readily find. A lengthy search for Scriptures in the middle of a prayer time can be distracting to your partner and can sometimes squelch what might otherwise have been a special time of closeness with the Lord.

Suggestions for Advance Preparation

1. Read the exercise, including its introduction, before actually using it, so that you are prepared to respond to the topic.

2. A list of suggested materials is included in each exercise. Gather what you need ahead of time so that you are ready to pray at the agreed-upon time.

3. Because Scripture is incorporated into the exercises, it is helpful, prior to the actual prayer time, to look up and note Scriptures related to the exercise. A topical concordance is invaluable for this.

4. Plan ahead for using any music or other aids desired to enhance the specific exercise.

5. Keep paper and pen handy during actual prayer time. When thoughts come to you, but they need to wait for the right opening or time, you can quickly jot them down for later use. Briefly capture significant experiences that occur during the prayer time so that they can be explored later. Those who enjoy journaling may want to keep a special couple prayer journal, but don't let writing interrupt the momentum of the prayer time. Do your journaling after the debriefing and on your own time.

6. Some of the exercises, especially those aimed at deeper intimacy, may require individual preparation, spiritually and emotionally. If there are significant trust or communication problems in your relationship, the deeper levels of couple prayer may be uncomfortable, and this discomfort needs to be addressed prior to attempting those exercises. Additional information and pointers are included with each exercise that may help address some of these issues.

Completing the Exercises

1. *Completing the evaluation form and debriefing*: Each exercise concludes with the completion of an evaluation form. We found it helpful to do this together on one form, which allowed us to discuss the prayer session and minimize the writing. For some, it may be easier or more helpful for each spouse to complete a form independently and then get together to discuss the results.

    It is especially important to note what needs to be done differently to improve the quality of prayer time for both of you. We kept extra paper available during this debriefing to jot down especially important or meaningful insights gained from the prayer time, which led to further exploration of Scripture or whatever the Holy Spirit seemed to be leading us to pursue in more depth.

2. *Discernment*: Vitally important to any spiritual experience is the need to discern whether what happened is from God, as opposed to your own doing or even the Enemy's. This is dealt with in more depth on pages 32-34, but is emphasized because of its importance.

    The five basic questions to ask of your prayer experience are included briefly here as a reminder that the exercise is not complete without this step, which is included in every evaluation form at the end of each exercise.

    *   Does it glorify God?
    *   Does it conform to the doctrine of Christ?
    *   Does it conform to God's Word?
    *   Does it result in a character that is godly?
    *   Are your spouse or other Holy Spirit-filled believers in spiritual agreement?

The Evaluation Form for Prayer Exercises

Following is an explanation of the categories found on the evaluation form for each exercise.

1. Physical Experience

     This area includes the most mundane of physical things, such as pain from an uncomfortable body position to interruptions from the telephone ringing. Fatigue is a major and too-common cause of poor quality time and focus on prayer. It cannot be said often enough that you must make this time such a high priority that other things are not allowed to crowd your couple prayer time out. Waiting until all else is done will leave either no time or exhaustion that prevents a quality experience.

     Plan for improvement: This should include changing those physical and environmental things that distracted you from being fully focused on prayer. Write out whatever changes will be needed to improve the next prayer date, and review your plan before that date.

2. Emotional Experience

     This area includes your attitude and how you felt during the experience. Attitude is something that needs to be personally checked and adjusted accordingly, prior to your prayer date. If "unfinished business" is affecting your attitude, it will impact your prayer time. Deal with this first, even if it means canceling your prayer date and rescheduling.

     There is a reason that God provided partitioned areas, in both the tabernacle and the temple, that preceded one's entering the Holy of Holies. One of these areas included a basin in which to wash so that intimacy with God would not be inhibited by "dirty flesh."
Feelings experienced during the prayer time should be noted and discussed during debriefing after your prayer time, as explained in the introduction.

     Plan for improvement: If your emotional experience was either positive or negative, both should be noted. Hang on to what worked, and write out changes needed for what did not work well. Sometimes surprise feelings result even in an atmosphere that does not need changing, but they are worth noting as insightful, as you may be led to explore them further, either on your own or with your spouse.

3. Spiritual Experience

     This area is harder to define, as it overlaps all other areas. What you are looking for, specific to this area, is your experience of God in whatever way He manifested Himself. Sometimes it is in silence, which can incorrectly be interpreted as an absence of His presence. Since, in both the Old and New Testaments, God promised never to leave or forsake us, we can be assured that He is present with us. Silence on God's part may have nothing to do with you, in terms of inhibiting God, as He demonstrates silences throughout the Bible and even commands us to be silent before Him at times.

However, there may be reasons that you can identify that would hinder or prevent Him from speaking to you. These may include a lack of focus on Him due to distractions, fatigue, or other things already mentioned above. If so, these things should be identified and included in your plan for improvement, even if they are already identified in other sections.

God connects to each of us in our own uniqueness: every sheep hears His voice but not in the same way. In the book of Acts, the miracle of understanding and hearing God did not occur through an unrecognizable language spoken by those who were filled with the Holy Spirit. It is clear that the crowd of listeners heard God's message in their *own, native languages.*

You and your spouse may have different experiences with God, and both of you will gain something in sharing those differences, both positive and negative. Usually, a negative spiritual experience occurs when others have expectations and place limitations on how God may choose to relate to us. Then, when our experience does not fit "in the box," we receive the message—overtly or covertly—that our understanding or experience of God is wrong. Remember to check the steps of discernment again, and pray for the Holy Spirit to lead you to truth, not other people.

Plan for improvement: If your spiritual experience was either positive or negative, it should be noted. Hang on to what worked, and write out changes needed for what did not work well. Sometimes there are surprise experiences that do not need changing, but merely noting them can be insightful. Often these experiences can lead to further exploration, either individually or together. Jotting down quick notes is particularly valuable for this reason, which is why prayer does not restrict itself to closed eyes. Ears opened to God, not closed eyes, are the key to hearing Him.

4. Relationship Experience

This area may overlap with your emotional and spiritual experience. What you are looking for, specific to this area, is how you perceived your experience *with* your spouse, not independent of him or her. This is the hardest area to deal with when praying with anyone, let alone your spouse. Given the premise that your relationship will grow as you struggle for true intimacy with one another in prayer, it is vitally important that you identify and be honest about this aspect of your prayer experience. Just as regular conversation and communication is very difficult, at best—and sometimes completely impossible, at worst—expect that you may have more negative feelings at first.

After you have identified specific behaviors that are the source of the difficulties, it is then possible to make plans for improvement. Please refer to the Conflict Resolution Script in the section on communication to help you frame the experience from your own perspective, taking ownership for your own feelings and presenting a constructive solution.

Plan for improvement: Based on the above, write out your plan for improvement in the form of a proposal or option worth trying, leaving room for the possibility that other options offered by your spouse may have equal worth. In any case, be willing to let go of what does not work well, and hang on to what does work well.

5. Discernment of Experience

This step is elaborated on in the following section, but suffice it to say that your prayer time will only be wholesome and growth-promoting if God's Spirit is the one present and presiding, rather than flesh or even demonic spirits. Do not be tempted to skip this step, as it is vital to your growth in spiritual intimacy as a couple. Use the following section to aid you in this process. Look up the Scriptures associated with each test, because they reveal the nature of God and His Spirit.

Plan for improvement: Based on the above, evaluate how well your experience lines up with the five tests listed in the section below. Because the bottom line is experiencing God's love and giving God's love to one another, it will correlate with your overall experience of the exercise.

Discernment: Why and How to Test Whether Something Is from God

Scripture teaches us that we should bring our experiences, especially spiritual ones, to Scripture for testing (John 5:39, 2 Timothy 3:16–17, 1 John 4:1). Debriefing the experience of praying together is a very important step that should not be overlooked. It will keep each partner accountable to the other, as well as both of you accountable to God, as you grow in spiritual intimacy with one another and with God. Accountability is important for several reasons:

- Holding the experience up to Scripture will allow exposure to the light of truth, preventing experiences from leading us astray.
- Holding the experience up to Scripture in its correct context will expose abuse of Scripture and using Scripture to abuse others.
- Holding the experience up to Scripture as the plumb line against which all else is measured will allow for correction of praying amiss, contrary to the will of God.
- Holding the experience up to the Word of God will cause new growth and intimacy with God and one another.

The steps of discernment ask the following test questions of your experience:

1. Does the experience glorify God (Romans 15:1–7), witnessed by the presence of His Spirit (1 John 4:12–13)?
2. Does the experience conform to the doctrine of *Christ*, who conformed to the image of God's love (John 15:8–13), as opposed to man's or a given church's doctrine (2 John vv. 7–9; 1 John 4:1–3)?
3. Does the experience conform to God's Word in correct context (1 John 4:7–13; 2 Timothy 3:16)?
4. Does the experience result in a character that is godly (James 3:13–18)? This step may take time before some objective, observable results are evident, but in the context of prayer with your spouse, most of the characteristics should be evident during the prayer time.
5. Are your spouse or other Holy Spirit-filled believers in spiritual agreement about what happened (Proverbs 1:5; 11:15; 12:15; 27:9)? First, is your spouse in spiritual agreement with you about the experience? If there is confusion or uncertainty, check out your experience with other trusted believers. Be sure that the two of you are in agreement about sharing your intimate prayer experience with someone else.

These five steps will be needed for the evaluation form that follows each prayer exercise, so you may want to mark this page to refer back to.

Any Scripture can be taken out of the context of its particular passage or the Bible as a whole. At the very least, this generally results in the misapplication of Scripture in a given situation. At worst, it results in spiritual abuse of one another. If your motive in praying with your spouse is to change your spouse in any way, you will most certainly become guilty of spiritual abuse through misapplication of Scripture, as well as misapplication of prayer.

God's Word is the sword of correction for our own hearts, not the hearts of others. Prayer, like any other interaction between people, can be manipulative through hidden agendas. God tells us in His Word that misplaced prayers will not be heard or answered (James 4:2b–3).

While the discernment process can be time-consuming and may need extra time beyond the planned prayer time, the next exercise should probably wait for scheduling until you have taken the time and effort to debrief as outlined here. We live in a quick-fix culture that does not teach us to study Scripture in context and then to correctly apply it to the situation (2 Timothy 2:15). If you are unfamiliar with Scripture or do not study your Bible regularly, this will take more time, but even a beginner can mine the Word of God and come up with exciting discoveries.

We have found that no matter how familiar we are with the Bible passages, the Holy Spirit is absolutely necessary for revealing the truths of Scripture as needed for particular application in each experience. Prayer definitely needs to be applied to this step, asking the Holy Spirit to guide you and lead you to all truth (John 16:13). One of the many advantages to preparing ahead of time for a given prayer exercise is that relevant Scriptures can be located and studied individually. Then the actual prayer time is more likely to be consistent with God's Word, thus already completing some of the steps of discernment ahead of time.

Chapter 3

Participation on the Journey

Preface to Prayer Exercise 1: Acknowledging and Honoring God, Our Father

One of the easiest and least threatening ways to come together in unity in prayer is to focus on God rather than each other. For this reason, the first exercise focuses exclusively on God and His attributes, not the least of which are His holiness and the fact that He is our heavenly Father. Use of a topical concordance is an easy way to look up names and attributes of God, and there are whole books dedicated to the names of God as they appear in Scripture.

In preparation for this exercise, we compiled a list of names and attributes of God so that we could use it in this exercise. There is no better way to know God than through studying His Word, which is a love letter to us from beginning to end. In His Word He makes His character and nature known, and it is impossible to know whether your understanding of God is based in truth unless you check that understanding against Scripture.

We have designed each prayer session to include a time for debriefing. This is to be a time of discerning what the Holy Spirit did and what you experienced. A key test in discernment is whether the experience is grounded in and consistent with God's Word. There are many Scriptures noted throughout this book, and we encourage you to look them up and read them in context.

God resides in the praises of His people (Psalm 22:3), and this exercise is an opportunity for you and your mate to praise and thank Him for who He is. Think of this time as an opportunity to celebrate "Father's Day" with the understanding that He loves you and desires that you know Him intimately, just as He knows you intimately. Your love for Him will be in direct proportion to the knowledge and understanding you have of Him. The greater your knowledge and understanding of how He loves you, the greater your capacity for experiencing, recognizing, and responding to His love.

If you find yourself unsure of whether God really loves you, this exercise should help you see just how many ways He demonstrates His love to you, because His nature is love. Every name and attribute of God in Scripture is a reflection of His love toward all of His creation, especially those of us who belong to Him. As you explore Scripture, be sure to note the context of His specific attributes and character. While He is merciful to those who are in covenant with Him, He is also just, and like a good parent, He disciplines His children. He is also ruthless in dealing with His enemies. If you struggle with certain attributes of God, such as His anger, study the context in Scripture where He expresses anger, so you will learn from Him about how He expresses perfect love, even in anger.

As you learn more about God, who is perfect love (1 John 4:16), we hope that you will learn to love both God and one another in new and deeper ways. We found this rather simple exercise to be a pleasant surprise, as God truly did inhabit our praises, and the Holy Spirit surrounded us with a sense of deep peace and love. We were surprised that we lost all track of time. There seems to be no end to the ways we have individually experienced God's love, expressed in His different names and attributes. An hour quickly passed without our notice, so, for the sake of completing the exercise—including the evaluation and debriefing—we cut it off. If you agreed to limit the time at the outset, be prepared to revise your time frame, but remember to go with the comfort level of whichever spouse does not want to continue.

This exercise could easily be repeated before moving on to the next level of prayer together. It is also a good exercise to return to as you move to deeper levels that may be much more challenging than this one. Sometimes moving to deeper levels in unfamiliar, intimate relationship territory is like moving out into unfamiliar deep water: you may need to back up to a shallower level if moving deeper is too scary on the first try. Feel free to take a step backward if needed before moving ahead, as God cherishes any effort you make to commune with Him.

The next exercise is also in shallow water where you can still see the bottom, so we encourage you to plunge in with all four feet, without worrying that you will be in over your heads. While all of the exercises are meant to be completed in their original order, you may want to repeat this first one often, or even include it as a preface to another exercise.

Indeed, how wonderful it is when we are in living in unity with one another and with Him (Psalm 133:1). Praising our Father together raises us up in unity with Christ to sit with him in heaven (Ephesians 2:6), far out of reach of the Enemy who seeks to destroy our marriages.

Prayer Exercise 1

"Our Father in heaven, may we honor your holy name."
Acknowledge God, our Father, with praise and thanksgiving.

Purpose
- To acknowledge and honor the character of God, your heavenly Father
- To invite Jesus to join you in worshipping God
- To ask the Holy Spirit to give you prayers that are an aroma pleasing to God
- To establish a safe base for praying together in unity and to set the stage for building deeper prayer intimacy as a couple

Helpful Materials
- Bible
- concordance
- notebook/paper and pens
- sacred music that enhances prayer
- list of names/attributes of Father God, made prior to your prayer time

Process
1. Taking turns at least once, open in prayer by dedicating this time to God, your heavenly Father. Invite God's Son, Jesus, to join you in praising your Father, given his promise in Matthew 18:20. Ask the Holy Spirit to speak to you and through you, drawing you in unity before the Father's throne.

2. Take time in silence to focus on the attributes of God, especially those that are meaningful to you personally, as well as in relation to your spouse and marriage. Make notes during this time, as it will be helpful during the next step.

3. Take turns speaking out a prayer of praise for one attribute at a time. Use Scripture that relates to attributes and names of God, incorporating it into a prayer of thanksgiving for that attribute.
   Here's an example of Scripture-based prayer:

   Verse: God's nature is love (1 John 4:16)
   Prayer: "Thank you, God, for being a loving Father."

4. Taking at least one turn each, pray out a closing statement of thanks for this prayer time, knowing that God, your Father, delights in your praises of Him.

5. Together or separately, complete the evaluation form and debrief with each other, focusing on what went well and what needs improvement. Don't skip the steps for discernment to evaluate the experience against Scripture as your guide, especially if words were spoken or feelings and thoughts arose that created doubt or confusion. Note on the evaluation form your plans for improvement for the next session. Using a notebook for journaling, take notes on significant aspects and insights that may be worth pursuing.

6. Set up the next appointment to meet with Jesus together in prayer. It may be helpful to read through the exercise ahead of time so that any advance preparation can be done prior to the appointment.

Prayer Exercise 1: Evaluation Form

1. Physical Experience:

   Plan for Improvement:

2. Emotional Experience:

   Plan for Improvement:

3. Spiritual Experience:

   Plan for Improvement:

4. Relationship Experience:

   Plan for Improvement:

5. Discernment of Experience:
   - Does it glorify God?
   - Does it conform to the doctrine of Christ?
   - Does it conform to God's Word?
   - Does it result in a character that is godly?
   - Are your spouse or other Holy Spirit-filled believers in spiritual agreement?

   Plan for Improvement:

6. Next Appointment:

Preface to Prayer Exercise 2: God's Kingdom on Earth

It is easy to think of God's kingdom being established in heaven because many hymns and church teachings speak of heaven as a perfect place, separate from earth, not bound by the limitations and imperfections of life on earth. Scripture, however, speaks of the kingdom that has come to earth through Jesus Christ (Matthew 2:1–2; Matthew 6:33; Mark 1:14–15), and the Lord's Prayer specifically mentions asking for God's kingdom to come to earth, just as it already is in heaven.

This exercise is designed to help you see that God is the provider of all that is good and perfect (James 1:17) and that He does not withhold these gifts before we get to heaven. His desire is for us to experience His goodness now, and one of the institutions He established on earth so that we can experience His kingdom now is marriage. In fact, there are gifts that He gives us on earth through marriage that He does not give in heaven, since He states that there will be no marriages in heaven as we have on earth. The only marriage in heaven that we will experience is the marriage of the Lamb, Jesus Christ, to his believers, the church (Matthew 22:29–30; Revelation 19:7–9).

Rather than focusing on marriage itself as a gift, this exercise focuses on identifying the individual gifts you each possess and bring to your marriage. (The final two exercises deal with praise and thanksgiving specifically for your marriage itself.) If you have been married for many years or have gotten to a place where you have lost sight of the original gifts you saw in your partner, this exercise is a good opportunity to reaffirm your mate while reminding yourself of the gifts God has given you through your mate.

Using the admonition in Revelation 2:4, consider your ultimate love, Jesus, and then look for his qualities mirrored in your mate. Every attribute in your spouse that imitates Christ is a gift to you from God, your heavenly father. This exercise focuses on building up one another.

In preparation for it, make a list of the attributes in your mate that are God's gift to you. The goal here is not to make a wish list. The list should be a reality list of Christlike qualities that are already present, regardless of how frequently or infrequently your mate displays them. Be careful not to use this prayer exercise to send "fix-it" messages to your spouse, such as, "Lord, thank you for the one time my mate showed your servanthood when he did the dishes." If you are struggling to identify specific characteristics of Christlikeness in your mate, look up Scriptures about Christ and learn what he blesses or approves of. Matthew 5–7 is a good place to start.

None of us demonstrate God's character with total consistency, and if you are at a very strained point in your marriage, it may be really hard to see in your mate even a few of the attributes in Scripture that pertain to the nature and character of love, Christ, God, and godly men and women. Especially if you are struggling in your marriage, prepare for this exercise in advance through your own individual prayer time. Get alone with God, and ask Him through the Holy Spirit to reveal what, in your character, reflects Christ and what does not, especially in relation to your mate. God's kingdom will only come to earth in your marriage to the degree that you are willing to conform to the image of Christ.

After your prayer time together using this exercise, you may have new insight into how your spouse sees and experiences you. Use this insight as a guide for praying about those areas where you need to be more Christlike to your mate. You need to thank God for the attributes your mate identifies in you as Christlike, because God, not you, produces His character fruit in your life.

As we were developing the exercises and using ourselves for the first test run, we gained some helpful experiences that we will pass on to you. First, prepare in advance for all the exercises so that your prayer time will flow more smoothly. Often the Holy Spirit, who promises to reveal all truth to you (John 16:13), will prompt you to seek out His Word on the subject at hand during prayer. (Many of the Scriptures included in this book came to us via the Holy Spirit during our test runs of the exercises.)

Second, make sure that you are physically rested and well. Wayne is a diabetic, and he was struggling with low blood sugar during this exercise, which greatly compromised his ability to focus and put energy into it. Our *plan for improvement* on the evaluation form definitely included making sure we were both physically, mentally, and emotionally up for the task.

An interesting thing happened to Wayne during this exercise. He found it difficult to think of God's gifts in our marriage as being divisible into those belonging separately to him and to Jan. It is not that he fails to see Jan as a unique individual, but we have been spiritually close for so long that it seemed awkward to try to view God's gifts as separately given to each of us. It is vitally important, however, to be able to build up one another through recognition of each other's individual uniqueness.

Unless this individual recognition happens, many negative outcomes are possible, not the least of which is a spouse feeling taken for granted, not valued, and not loved. Assumptions are always dangerous, and speaking for both you and your spouse when you thank God for a godly marriage is presumptuous—unless you have both discussed your agreement on this point.

Focusing on the marriage apart from your individual, unique gifts is a way to avoid intimacy. At this stage, the development of intimacy in prayer requires that you explicitly acknowledge the unique giftings God has bestowed on each of you.

Prayer Exercise 2

"May your kingdom come on earth to us now."
Acknowledge marriage as a holy institution. Offer praise and thanksgiving for each other as a gift from our Father.

Purpose
- To acknowledge that your marriage is a holy gift from your Father, that you might experience His kingdom on earth
- To invite Jesus to join you in thanking your Father for the gift of your marriage and specifically for your mate
- To ask the Holy Spirit to reveal to you the gifts God has given to you in each other
- To establish a safe base for building up one another and setting the stage for building deeper spiritual intimacy as a couple

Helpful Materials
- Bible
- concordance
- notebook/paper and pens
- copy of wedding vows, if you have them. If not, use the traditional vows in Appendix 2 or write your own.
- sacred music related to marriage that enhances prayer
- list of relevant Scriptures

Process
1. Taking turns in prayer, dedicate this time to God, asking the Holy Spirit to speak to you and through you how you are to build up one another through praise and thanksgiving to God for one another. Let Jesus' presence remind you that He is agreeing with you and interceding to the Father for your marriage (Hebrews 7:25).

2. Take time to be silent, and allow the Holy Spirit to speak to you about what God has given you in each other. Ask the Holy Spirit to show you how to express the instruction in 1 Thessalonians 5:11 to build up one another. Take notes during this time to assist you during prayer.

3. Take turns speaking out a praise for one gift at a time, alternating with each other. Make note of the gifts your spouse sees in you. Use Scriptures that relate to men and women, husbands and wives, with a focus on positive attributes you see in your mate. Then speak them out as prayer offerings.

Here's an example of Scripture-based prayer:

Verse: Love that is from God is patient and kind (1 Corinthians 13:4).
Prayer: "Father, I thank you for my mate's patience and kindness."

4. If you have a copy of your wedding vows, speak them out to each other in a new commitment. If you do not have the original words of your vows, there are traditional and sample Christian vows in Appendix 2, or you can write your own. Taking turns, close out your prayer time with thanksgiving for the sanctity of marriage as God has ordered it, and thank your Father for each other.

5. Together or separately, complete the evaluation form and debrief with each other, focusing on what went well and what needs improvement. Don't skip the steps for discernment to evaluate the experience against Scripture as your guide, especially if words were spoken or feelings and thoughts arose that created doubt or confusion. Note on the evaluation form your plans for improvement for the next session. Using a notebook for journaling, take notes on significant aspects and insights that may be worth pursuing.

6. Set up the next appointment to meet with Jesus together in prayer. It may be helpful to read through the exercise ahead of time so that any advance preparation can be done prior to the appointment.

Prayer Exercise 2: Evaluation Form

1. Physical Experience:

    Plan for Improvement:

2. Emotional Experience:

    Plan for Improvement:

3. Spiritual Experience:

    Plan for Improvement:

4. Relationship Experience:

    Plan for Improvement:

5. Discernment of Experience:
    *   Does it glorify God?
    *   Does it conform to the doctrine of Christ?
    *   Does it conform to God's Word?
    *   Does it result in a character that is godly?
    *   Are your spouse or other Holy Spirit-filled believers in spiritual agreement?

    Plan for Improvement:

6. Next Appointment:

Preface to Prayer Exercise 3: Blessing One Another According to God's Will

When we think of praying for God's will to be done through us on earth, we frequently think of something hard, unpleasant, and sacrificial. While this may be true at times, the focus in this exercise is on the very pleasant task of being obedient through blessing one another. The covenant God made with Abraham was to bless Abraham so that he would be a blessing to others (Genesis 12:2). Likewise, God is consistent throughout the Old and New Testaments in His desire to bless us so that we can bless one another.

We are, in fact, commanded to bless rather than curse one another, even our enemies (Matthew 5:44). Blessing our enemies may be very difficult, but in the context of marriage, it should be a very pleasant command to bless our mates. Before continuing, let's take a look at what the act of blessing involves. God, our Father, demonstrates His definition of this act through His own example:

- God blesses us by providing us with His power, giving us the ability to succeed in accomplishing what He has called us to do (John 1:12; Acts 1:8; 2 Corinthians 9:8; Philippians 1:6).
- God blesses us by providing us with His abundant life (Matthew 7:11; John 10:10; John 15:11).
- God blesses us by providing His total peace (Isaiah 26:3; John 14:27; Philippians 4:7).
- God blesses us by providing His Word, which contains all the promises of His goodness toward us. He chooses and desires to bless us (2 Corinthians 1:20).
- God blesses us through giving us Jesus Christ as the blessing that touches every area of our life, spelled out in the third chapter of Galatians.

When we look at how much God desires to bless us, we can get a sense of what we are to desire for each other. A safe place to start the process of blessing one another is in prayers of blessing, where we ask God to bless our beloved based on His Scripture promises. The Bible writes of the infinite blessings that God has for us as His children.

This exercise focuses on this specific act of blessing, because it is safe and nonthreatening. We do not need to try to produce any goodness from ourselves to bestow on our mates. We also do not need to feel "worthy enough" to receive God's blessings. Our only worthiness to receive the goodness of God, our Father, comes through the perfect sacrifice of His Son, not our own efforts. We receive by faith the grace we do not deserve.

We also need to use God's model of blessing to bless one another beyond this first safe and undemanding step of prayer. We need to understand the act of blessing by looking to Scripture for revelation. Being a living blessing through our actions mirrors the promises of

God. Beyond numerous examples throughout Scripture that support God's transfer of His love through His people to others, Jesus is the ultimate example and teacher of being blessed in order to bless others.

The Beatitudes and similitudes from the Sermon on the Mount are just one example of Jesus' teachings about how we are to live as channels of blessing to others (Matthew 5:1–16). In his command to love each other as he has loved us (John 15:12), Jesus summed up all that he showed us. Known as the "Prayer of St. Francis of Assisi," this anonymous but well-known prayer is a model for converting *words* of blessing into *actions* of blessing.

> Lord, make me an instrument of your peace.
> Where there is hatred, let me sow love,
> Where there is doubt, faith,
> Where there is sadness, joy.
> O Divine Master,
> Grant that I may not so much seek to be consoled as to console,
> To be understood as to understand,
> To be loved as to love.
> For it is in giving that we receive.
> It is in pardoning that we are pardoned.
> It is in dying that we are born to eternal life.

Our prayer for you is that you would spend time individually at the feet of Jesus in prayer, asking to be conformed to his image. Some of the exercises that follow (specifically, numbers 6, 7, and 8) will present you with the opportunity to engage each other as prayer partners for the purpose of conforming your lives to that of Christ so that you can move beyond praying for God's blessings on your spouse to being a living blessing to your spouse.

Prayer Exercise 3

"May your kingdom come, through your will being done."
Submit to the will of our Father by blessing one another.

Purpose
- To pray according to the will of the Father, with the scriptural command to bless one another (1 Peter 3:9)
- To experience the will of the Father as loving and nonthreatening
- To create a safe and positive beginning to moving into deeper prayer intimacy

Helpful Materials
- Bible
- concordance
- notebook/paper and pens
- sacred music that enhances prayer
- list of promises and blessings for us in Scripture

Process
1. In prayer, with each partner taking at least one turn, dedicate this prayer time to God. Ask Jesus to join you and perfect your prayers before your Father. Ask the Holy Spirit to teach you through Jesus' example of submitting to his Father's will.

2. Take time in silence to focus on your Father, the source of all blessings, and ask the Holy Spirit to reveal blessings He desires you to pray over your mate.

3. Take turns praying out a blessing from your Father over your spouse. Take as much time as you need for this because you are giving a gift to your spouse. Use Scriptures that contain God's blessings and promises for His children, converting them to a prayer over one another.

   Here's an example of Scripture-based prayer:

   Verse: You, God, will keep me perfectly at peace when my mind is focused on you (Isaiah 26:3).
   Prayer: "Father, I ask You to bless my mate with a continual sense of Your presence so that (s)he may be focused on You and blessed with Your continual peace."

4. When both of you have exchanged blessings and are ready to close this time of prayer, each of you take at least one turn speaking out a final prayer of thanksgiving.

5. Together or separately, complete the evaluation form and debrief with each other, focusing on what went well and what needs improvement. Don't skip the steps for discernment to evaluate the experience against Scripture as your guide, especially if words were spoken or feelings and thoughts arose that created doubt or confusion. Note on the evaluation form your plans for improvement for the next session. Using a notebook for journaling, take notes on significant aspects and insights that may be worth pursuing.

6. Set up the next appointment to meet with Jesus together in prayer. It may be helpful to read through the exercise ahead of time so that any advance preparation can be done prior to the appointment.

Prayer Exercise 3: Evaluation Form

1. Physical Experience:

   Plan for Improvement:

2. Emotional Experience:

   Plan for Improvement:

3. Spiritual Experience:

   Plan for Improvement:

4. Relationship Experience:

   Plan for Improvement:

5. Discernment of Experience:
   - Does it glorify God?
   - Does it conform to the doctrine of Christ?
   - Does it conform to God's Word?
   - Does it result in a character that is godly?
   - Are your spouse or other Holy Spirit-filled believers in spiritual agreement?

   Plan for Improvement:

6. Next Appointment:

Preface to Prayer Exercise 4: Submission to Jesus Christ as the Head of Our Marriage

One of the most misunderstood and misapplied areas of Scripture is in the area of submission. Most Christians understand the doctrine and concept of submission to Jesus Christ as Lord, even as we struggle to live that out. But when it comes to teaching in Scripture concerning submission to one another, especially wives to their husbands, walls of resistance go up. This is a human reaction based on our own unwillingness to let anyone rule over us, given that we are by nature self-centered and rebellious against authority (Isaiah 14:12–14; Romans 7:14–17).

In addition, many of us have been spiritually abused by the misapplication of Scripture in this area, which has led to emotional and/or physical abuse. The focus on this exercise is on submitting yourselves and your marriage to Jesus Christ, not just because it defines Christian marriage (Ephesians 1:22–23; 5:31–32), but because he is safe to submit to. He is unable to abuse you, because he has God's very nature (Jeremiah 31:3; Romans 3:10; 1 John 4:16).

Unless each of you submits *individually* to Jesus Christ as your personal Lord, it will be impossible to submit your marriage to his headship. You each may need to spend time alone with God to deal with your own resistance to letting him rule over you. It is helpful to look at the perfect model of submission by exploring Scripture to learn about Jesus and his example of total submission to his Father. The book of John speaks clearly of this relationship, and much can be learned by reading it in its entirety, as it is a very personal account of Jesus' submission to God, the Father. This will help you understand what is required, what is at stake, and more importantly, what the rewards are.

You may be reluctant to allow God, the Father, or Jesus, the Son, to rule and reign in your life, because submitting to other human beings has led to abuse. If you find it hard to yield to your heavenly Father, you may need to consider whether you are projecting imperfect human attributes onto God, whose fatherhood is perfect. Jesus earned the right to reign over you through his perfect submission to his Father, but his headship is based in sacrificial servanthood (Ephesians 5:25–27).

We humans, being imperfect and lacking understanding of these perfect models, often misuse, misunderstand, and miss the mark due to wrong motives. God never requires submission to Him for His own selfish interests. He requires submission to Him because only He can give life in all of its abundance as a result of that submission. Jesus was in perfect submission to his Father's will so that all of us would have access to that life in the fullest and most eternal sense of the word. Giving up your life to God is how you gain it, not lose it (Mark 8:35).

The purpose of this exercise is to encourage the two of you to give your marriage to God, your Father. He instituted it for you and wants you to receive the fullness of His promises for life through this holy union. Jesus was given headship by God over your marriage, but he will not preside over it unless you ask him to. Wives, do not worry about the issue of submitting to your husband. The order in Scripture is clear concerning submission in marriage, and submitting to your husband is last in the order God has ordained.

First comes our individual submission to God our Father through Jesus Christ, then submission as spouses to one another, and then submission of wives to our husbands. Unless the first and second conditions are met, God cannot create the safe environment necessary for submission of a wife to her husband. Ephesians 5:17–33 covers this topic, especially the way the husband is to love his wife. Unless he strives to love her in the same way that Christ loves the church (and we as believers are the church), it is unreasonable for him to expect her to submit to him at all.

Husbands, remember that Jesus himself never demands or commands us to submit to him. Submission by definition requires voluntary yielding. A submission that is not completely voluntary is oppression. Submission is a process, and Jesus uses God's love to woo us, draw us, and call us to him so that we can trust him enough through his selflessness to give him our lives (Jeremiah 31:3). God does not call any of us to irrational surrender to Him. He proves first that He is trustworthy and worth surrendering our lives to (Lamentations 3:23), knowing that we need to believe He desires and plans to enrich us and not harm us (Jeremiah 29:11).

When we did this exercise, we were not struggling with submission—personally or in our marriage—which allowed the Holy Spirit to reveal profound truths in a passage of Scripture that has much to say to those who may be struggling with deep wounds, especially in the area of trusting God with their marriage.

We were praying for the Holy Spirit to show us God's heart for marriage and families. Wayne was led to Isaiah 54, which is an incredible picture of marriage, with God as the husband and Jerusalem as the wife. The storehouse of riches available to those who order their marriage after this chapter is far greater than what any man can offer his wife or his children. Apart from his own submission to God, the Father, no man can give his wife all that is in this Scripture. Only by his own submission to the Father can a husband be a conduit for God's love to pour out on his own wife and children.

If you are a woman who has been devastated, either in previous relationships or in your current marriage, look at all that God promises to restore to you through a godly husband who is fully submitted to God. Jan had claimed this passage of Scripture as her own after several devastating relationships where she experienced betrayal and abuse with Christian men. God gave her all that was promised in this chapter through her relationship with Jesus as her husband, and eventually He gave her a flesh-and-blood model of His love for her through a midlife marriage to Wayne.

We encourage both of you to submit your marriage to Christ as the head of your physical and spiritual union in this exercise, and then pray for God to pour out the rich rewards promised in Isaiah 54. Your list of blessings, prayed over each other in Exercise 3, will expand as you both grow in Christlikeness, which will naturally flow out of submission to Christ, the River of Life.

Prayer Exercise 4

"May your will be done on earth as it is in heaven."
Submit to our Father's will. Christ is God's appointed head of our marriage.

Purpose
- To submit your marriage to the will of God by agreeing to God's order
- To ask Jesus Christ to assume his rightful place as head of your marriage
- To begin moving to a deeper level of spiritual intimacy as a couple

Helpful Materials
- Bible
- concordance
- notebook/paper and pens
- sacred music that enhances prayer
- list of Scriptures related to submitting to God and one another

Process
1. Each of you take at least one brief turn to dedicate this prayer time to God, asking the Holy Spirit to speak to you and through you regarding the process of submission to your Father's will. Ask Jesus to guide you through the Holy Spirit to his life example of perfect submission to his Father (Luke 23:46).

2. Take time to be silent, waiting expectantly for the Holy Spirit to speak to you about the act of submission to Jesus as Lord. Take notes to facilitate actual prayer time.

3. Take turns speaking out what you have been given by the Holy Spirit to teach you and lead you as an individual spouse and as a couple into acknowledgment of Jesus as head of your marriage. Look up Scriptures that relate to submitting and relinquishing your lives to God. Look up Scriptures that relate to submitting one to another according to the will of God. Use the Scriptures as a prayer offering.

    Here's an example of Scripture-based prayer:

    Verse: You are our Creator God. We are like clay in your hand (Isaiah 64:8).
    Prayer: "Father, I give you my life as a lump of soft clay, for you to mold and fashion as you will. Mold me into a fit helpmate to my partner, according to your will."

4. End the prayer time with each of you offering thanksgiving for the time in communion with Jesus in your midst, acknowledging Him as your individual head and as head of your marriage.

5. Together or separately, complete the evaluation form and debrief with each other, focusing on what went well and what needs improvement. Don't skip the steps for discernment to evaluate the experience against Scripture as your guide, especially if words were spoken or feelings and thoughts arose that created doubt or confusion. Note on the evaluation form your plans for improvement for the next session. Using a notebook for journaling, take notes on significant aspects and insights that may be worth pursuing.

6. Set up the next appointment to meet with Jesus together in prayer. It may be helpful to read through the exercise ahead of time so that any advance preparation can be done prior to the appointment.

Prayer Exercise 4: Evaluation Form

1. Physical Experience:

    Plan for Improvement:

2. Emotional Experience:

    Plan for Improvement:

3. Spiritual Experience:

    Plan for Improvement:

4. Relationship Experience:

    Plan for Improvement:

5. Discernment of Experience:
    *   Does it glorify God?
    *   Does it conform to the doctrine of Christ?
    *   Does it conform to God's Word?
    *   Does it result in a character that is godly?
    *   Are your spouse or other Holy Spirit-filled believers in spiritual agreement?

    Plan for Improvement:

6. Next Appointment:

Preface to Prayer Exercise 5: Asking Our Father to Meet Each Other's Needs

Even though Scripture states that God our Father knows our needs even before we ask (Matthew 6:8), He also invites us over and over again to ask Him specifically to meet our needs (Matthew 7:7–11; James 4:2). While this may seem like a contradiction, the reality is that God is no different than we are in His desire to communicate with those He loves. Just as your relationship with your mate would deteriorate if there were no meaningful communication between the two of you, so likewise our relationship with God deteriorates when there is no meaningful communication. The Lord's Prayer is our model for who, why, how and what God desires us to talk to Him about.

Even if it were possible to know all of your mate's needs, your relationship would be made weaker by your attempts to meet your mate's needs without their asking. It would be very presumptuous to attempt to meet the needs that you are so sure of without communication with your spouse about whether, when, and how he or she would like those needs met.

In His infinite wisdom, God knows our needs perfectly, but He does not force us to have a relationship with Him. He gives us complete freedom to either accept or reject any or all aspects of relationship with Him, even as He continues to pursue us with His love forever (Jeremiah 31:3; John 3:16; John 15:16; Romans 8:35, 37, 39).

God desires that we willingly ask and receive all that He has for us. He is our model for our relationship with our spouse, in that we should seek to be unpresumptuous in our marriage. We should seek to give up our expectations of each other in order that our mate feel loved and safe enough to freely ask and receive all that we have to give them. That level of trust in an earthly relationship is rare, given our human weaknesses and inadequacies. By the time we are adults, most of us have experienced enough wounds and failures in attempting to get our needs met by other human beings that we have learned not to trust others with meeting our needs.

The focus in this exercise, however, is less risky than asking our mates to meet our needs, because the focus is on asking God to meet our spouse's needs. In this exercise, we simply express our needs and ask our spouse to intercede for us before the Lord, our provider. While we are perfectly capable, through our own prayers, of asking God to meet our needs, it is appropriate to ask our mates to pray for us, because it allows our mate into our life.

By sharing our felt needs with one another, we expand the spiritual and emotional base of our marriage. Scripture enjoins us to carry one another's burdens (Galatians 6:2). A need shared is a burden made lighter, for in sharing we do not carry it alone. In asking our mate to petition our holy Father, who makes us whole to meet our needs, along with the ever-present Jesus, we create a tripod, which is a very stable base, joined together at the top by God. Trying to handle our needs alone is like a single stick attempting to remain upright without other supports. Even two sticks cannot form a stable base that will remain upright.

In our model prayer, asking for our daily bread is not limited to literal daily bread. We are created with physical, emotional, and spiritual needs that only God our Creator knows how best to meet. While it is possible to exist in a deprived state where we do not get what we need in these three areas on a daily basis, God desires that we experience more than lives of desperation and deprivation (John 10:10; Ephesians 3:14–21). If we are fed daily in all three of our areas of need, we are more than sustained. If we are fed a balanced and healthy diet in all three areas, we are supplied with the energy to grow rather than just to exist day to day. Sometimes we are in situations that throw our daily diets out of balance, and though we can maintain ourselves for short periods of time, we suffer ill effects in the long run.

The Israelites spent forty years in the desert, learning, among other things, how to rely on their God to meet their physical, emotional, and spiritual needs through daily outpourings from Him. In fact, if they tried to store up extra food from what God provided, this showed a lack of faith that He would do as He said and be their daily provision—and the additional food rotted. God wanted them to focus on one day at a time, trusting Him and not dwelling on what lay behind or worrying about what lay ahead. As they failed to look to God for their emotional and spiritual well-being daily, they became cantankerous, angry, bitter, selfish, stubborn, and obstinate—and any number of other adjectives that are the evidence of emotional disorder. Spiritually, they lost sight of God altogether as their provider and made an idol that had no ability to provide anything.

The Bible speaks often about daily routine related to all three areas of our human need. God built within us the very rhythm of our lives, centered around twenty-four-hour days, and it is no accident that we order our lives around twenty-four-hour time periods. Trying to escape the God-given twenty-four -hour cycle results in many negative consequences, which can be seen most immediately in the physical realm. Just missing food, water, and sleep for one day has profound negative effects on our bodies, and ultimately on our minds and spirits as well. Man does not live just by daily bread for his body; he needs every word that comes from God's mouth to live (Deuteronomy 8:3; Luke 4:4). We have emotional and spiritual needs that only God can meet, as well as physical needs, and God provides for all of them, day by day, as we ask for all that we need for today.

Prior to doing this exercise, several things need to be clarified. First, it is important to address the issue of *needs* versus *wants*. God does not promise to meet our wants; He promises to meet our every need. So it is important in preparation for this exercise to clarify whether you are asking based on need or want. Sometimes they are the same, such as "I want more of God in my life." In reality, this is also a need.

Second, it is important to distinguish between our own individual need that is separate from our spouse's need. A statement such as "I need my spouse to be more loving, helpful, involved, etc.," is not focused on you, and it has no place in this prayer exercise. (Exercise 11 is designed to address this, and it follows all of the other exercises by intention.)

Third, the need should be specific. The above examples are very vague and miss the point of this exercise, which is to go to our Father with *very specific* requests on behalf of our spouse. When we did this exercise, we did not have any intense needs, for which we were grateful. We both have multiple medical problems, so Jan asked for specific prayer related to healing. Using Scripture as the basis for laying on of hands (Mark 16:18), Wayne prayed very specifically for pain and lack of stamina to be removed, as well as the underlying illness.

Even though the time spent in prayer was not intense or deeply moving, there was a clear recognition that the unmet needs of one another impact us both. This exercise showed us that just as our physical needs affect us both, our time in prayer over those physical needs quickened our awareness and sensitivity to our spiritual connection as well. Jan's experience of being prayed over by Wayne felt very comforting and caring, especially given that most of the time she keeps physical pain to herself. Wayne's experience was that this was prayer at a very basic level, but it was vitally necessary. We both became more aware of how little we pray specifically for each other unless there is a crisis. The more mundane daily needs are easily overlooked, and yet these are the very "daily bread" needs that God wants us to address.

Up to this point, the exercises have been drawing the two of you into relationship with each other through prayer in areas that were relatively safe and less risky. The focus has been on going to God, the Father, in prayer rather than focusing on asking each other for something.

Exercise 6 will move us directly into the area of relationship with our mates that is the most difficult but the most necessary if we are to have a healthy marriage. It focuses on asking for and receiving forgiveness. It may be helpful to repeat this fifth exercise before moving to the next one, so you can feel more confident of a stronger sense of connection with your spouse in prayer. Having your mate directly pray over you is a way to experience love flowing from God through your spouse to you. Unless this is experienced first, you may not have built the foundation of love and safety needed for the deep, mutual growth in prayer that is intended for the next three exercises.

As mentioned previously, feel free to repeat any of the other prayer exercises before moving forward to these deeper and more challenging areas of prayer with your spouse.

Prayer Exercise 5

"Give us all that we need for today."
Ask our Father to meet each other's needs.

Purpose
- To acknowledge God as the source of meeting all of your needs
- To share your needs with your mate
- To hear your spouse acknowledge and demonstrate caring for you by petitioning your Father for your needs

Helpful Materials
- Bible
- concordance
- notebook/paper and pens
- sacred music that enhances prayer
- list of Scriptures related to God meeting our needs

Process
1. Praying in turn, dedicate this prayer time to God. Ask Jesus to agree with you before your Father to meet your every need. Ask the Holy Spirit to word your petitions perfectly in the throne room when you are not sure how best to pray.

2. In silence, focus on God as the only one who can perfectly meet your every need and acknowledge that expecting your spouse to meet all of your needs or yourself to meet all of your spouse's needs is not what God expects of you or how He designed marriage. Ask the Holy Spirit to reveal to you your real needs, asking for discernment from the Father as to whether your felt needs are in line with what He promises to provide. Take notes if it will help during prayer time with your spouse.

3. Take turns sharing a felt need. Then have your mate petition your Father to meet your need. Include physical, emotional, and spiritual needs. Keep notes regarding your mate's needs for future prayer support as well as for now. Use Scriptures that speak of needs, and turn them into prayers for each other. Here is an example of Scripture-based prayer:

    Verse: My God will meet all of your needs from His abundant riches (Philippians 4:19).

Prayer: "Thank you in advance, Father, for meeting my mate's need for an income sufficient for our family, knowing that you have promised to supply all our needs from your abundant riches."

4. Taking at least one turn each, close out your prayer time with thanksgiving for God's promises to meet your spouse's needs.

5. Together or separately, complete the evaluation form and debrief with each other, focusing on what went well and what needs improvement. Don't skip the steps for discernment to evaluate the experience against Scripture as your guide, especially if words were spoken or feelings and thoughts arose that created doubt or confusion. Note on the evaluation form your plans for improvement for the next session. Using a notebook for journaling, take notes on significant aspects and insights that may be worth pursuing.

6. Set up the next appointment to meet with Jesus together in prayer. It may be helpful to read through the exercise ahead of time so that any advance preparation can be done prior to the appointment.

Prayer Exercise 5: Evaluation Form

1. Physical Experience:

   Plan for Improvement:

2. Emotional Experience:

   Plan for Improvement:

3. Spiritual Experience:

   Plan for Improvement:

4. Relationship Experience:

   Plan for Improvement:

5. Discernment of Experience:
   • Does it glorify God?
   • Does it conform to the doctrine of Christ?
   • Does it conform to God's Word?
   • Does it result in a character that is godly?
   • Are your spouse or other Holy Spirit-filled believers in spiritual agreement?

   Plan for Improvement:

6. Next Appointment:

Preface to Prayer Exercise 6: Forgiveness from Our Father and Each Other

This exercise is probably the most difficult one, and advance preparation is needed if true healing, restoration, and deeper intimacy are to be achieved. There is certainly the potential for harm to be done, and the risks need to be assessed and weighed—for each of you individually and for both of you together—before moving ahead with this exercise. Just as there are certain aspects of physical and emotional intimacy that are not comfortable if no advance preparation has been made to ensure a positive experience, so it is the case for this step into deeper spiritual intimacy.

If you are in the habit of asking God to forgive you at the moment the Holy Spirit convicts you of sin, you may have already dealt with God for sins against your spouse. But unless you have gone to the one you have sinned against, intimacy will be blocked in two ways: (1) you may find yourself avoiding and creating distance between yourself and the person you have wronged, even if that person is unaware of your sin against them, and (2) the person wronged by you may draw away from you rather than confront you with his or her hurt.

When the wronged person is your spouse, it will hinder all three areas of intimacy—physical, emotional, and spiritual. Regardless of how close and intimate the relationship was before this barrier appeared, unless it is removed through the *complete* process of repentance to both God and your spouse *and* through reconciliation with both God and your spouse, the distance will almost certainly widen until the relationship itself may be over. Many married couples live very separated lives, where they are not intimately connected on any level, and this easily could be the result of unresolved hurts.

Jesus' washing of the disciples' feet in John 13:1–17 is a portrait of this level of intimacy. He acknowledged that the disciples were already clean because of their relationship to Him, just as we are "bathed" once and for all time when we accept his perfect blood sacrifice and enter into a relationship with him based on that gift of grace. However, just as sandals and dusty roads make foot washing a daily necessity if we want to keep our homes, and especially our beds, clean, our lives in this unclean world require constant "foot-washing."

Jesus is our model servant, showing us how to humble ourselves in service to one another. His act of foot-washing is also a wonderful picture of our cleansing one another by humbly forgiving each other often, knowing that God is faithful to forgive us as we forgive one another. Jesus ends his cleaning lesson with a promise: we will be blessed if we follow his example of humble servanthood. Forgiving and being forgiven are blessings of giving and receiving, and they further encourage the blessing of true intimacy, where we can be transparent with one another.

We hope you have been following the suggestions given in this book, especially in continually checking in with each other to make sure you are not moving ahead of one another or pushing one another faster or farther than both of you are comfortable with. You need, more than ever, to check with each other before doing this exercise. It should go without saying that coercion is anathema to an open, honest, and healthy relationship, but we are not always aware that we are pressuring someone to meet our expectations. Coercion in prayer, as in sex, eliminates the kind of mutual exchange of self that characterizes true intimacy. Forced nakedness in both sex and prayer results in shame and anger. On the other hand, mutual consent enhances the depth of both kinds of intimacy, because the two of you come together openly to share as much of yourselves as you can with each other.

While it may seem more romantic to have spontaneous intimacy, the reality is that true spontaneity and openness on the part of both partners only happens if a groundwork of mutual trust and understanding has been laid. Because our experience has been that most couples may lack experience praying together beyond the superficial, we feel that advance preparation for entering into a new level of spiritual intimacy will help make the experience a positive one.

Here are some of the questions you need to ask and answer before engaging in this exercise:

1. *Are you encouraging your mate to become spiritually intimate with you, or are you discouraging him or her through coercion or manipulation?*

    The person to ask, after yourself, is your spouse. If your mate is feeling pressured into this level of prayer, do not proceed with the exercise. Sometimes our own eagerness to move ahead is perceived by our mate as pressure. It might be helpful to talk about what is making the move to the next step uncomfortable for either one of you. It may be that the two of you need to continue praying together, using previous exercises that you completed comfortably, so that a broader base of trust can be established.

    One form of potential hindrance is "bargaining," as in "I'll risk confessing and forgiving you, if you do likewise." A better approach would be to let your spouse know, if you are ready to take the risk, that you are willing to start with a request for forgiveness—but that your mate does not have to feel obligated to respond in return. Continue to read the rest of the question and discussion sections below, as some of your concerns about this level of intimacy may be answered.

2. *Do you both share an understanding of what is asked, given, and received in the act of forgiveness?*

    If there is to be a restoration of relationship, forgiveness requires that both parties acknowledge the harm done. This means that both parties—the one asking for forgiveness for a specific harmful act, as well as the one in the position of granting forgiveness—need to see the act as harmful and not lightly dismiss it with "That's okay" or "Even though I do not understand what I did to hurt you, forgive me anyway."

Harming the one we love, whether accidental or intentional, is never "okay." The person seeking forgiveness should be seeking release of a burden that is real and not light, and the person in the position to grant or withhold that release needs to see the power he or she has to lighten a loved one's load. The one being asked for this gift is given the choice to set the other free, and he or she needs to understand that to give this gift means that there are no strings attached.

Asking for forgiveness means giving up the right to hold on to the wrong done against your mate, especially if you believe you are justified in doing the harm, and it means letting go of the wrong by forgiving yourself. Being asked to forgive means giving up the right to stay angry at your mate for that wrong done to you, even if you believe you are justified in your anger. This is a gift you also give yourself as the receiver of harm, because it frees you from harboring anger that can grow into bitterness and even hate. Unresolved anger acts as a cancer in both you and your marriage.

3. *Do you have a right motive for asking your spouse for forgiveness?*

If what you want is to be excused for your behavior, you do not understand the gift of forgiveness. Forgiveness is about genuine sorrow that you want your beloved to know you are experiencing for causing them pain. It is also about true repentance, where you make a 180-degree turn from your mistake and do not continue to repeat it. You may need to give your spouse permission to hold you accountable if this is a repetitive mistake. (See also the introductions to exercises 7 and 8.)

There may be some wrongs that you have done to your spouse that one or neither of you are ready to deal with at this time. Because these exercises are intended to help you grow in your prayer life together, it is not necessary to deal with extremely sensitive areas that one or both of you are uncomfortable discussing right now. Just as forgiveness is sometimes an extended process, so too is learning to pray together. In forgiveness, as in learning to pray together, the process goes more smoothly if it proceeds from the safe and familiar and builds from there.

Areas that would be safer to start with are outward behaviors that both you and your spouse are very aware of. These may include unkind or inconsiderate remarks or behaviors that you know offend your mate—such as sarcastic comments that your mate does not find amusing, or not picking up after yourself, hoping your spouse will do it for you if you leave it long enough. Every marriage provides ample opportunity for at least unintentionally taking each other for granted, and this is another relatively safe area to explore for practice in asking for and receiving forgiveness.

Be careful about your motive and the potential for your confession to injure your mate further, especially if the damage might be irreparable. If you are not sure how to handle a situation as severe as adultery or other actions that may destroy the trust base of your relationship, seek wise counsel with a trusted, mature Christian in an appropriate position to assist you, such as a pastor, friend of the same sex, or counselor.

4. *Does your spouse have your permission to say no to your request?*

Because it is actually a gift that you are asking for, requesting forgiveness from your mate is very much like asking for physical intimacy. He or she needs to be free to choose so that what you receive will be a gift given freely from the heart. You are asking your mate to give you release from guilt when they have been harmed by you, and they must be free to choose whether and when to give you that release.

In the context of teaching his disciples to pray (Matthew 6:14–15), Jesus clearly stated that we are to forgive one another—and that God will not forgive us our wrongs unless we do forgive others—but we are still free to choose whether and when we will do so. God will not violate us by taking away our freedom of choice, and we cannot claim to love one another if we violate each other by forcing the other person to conform to our will.

It may be helpful to write out your thoughts, attitudes, or actions that need forgiveness and give the items to your spouse to think about and decide whether and when he or she would be comfortable covering those issues with you in prayer together. If your spouse does not want to pray with you over a particular issue, ask him or her what would be the most helpful way to handle your request for forgiveness.

5. *What should I do if my mate declines my request?*

Respect your mate's decision, and treat your mate with the same love and respect that you would if he or she had granted you forgiveness. Show true repentance through a change in your actions, regardless of whether your mate has forgiven you for those actions. Unless there has been enough time allowed for working on an honest response, the asking may create an additional burden for both of you until your mate is ready and willing to forgive you.

Remember that God has already forgiven you the moment you confessed and asked Him to. His forgiveness is not conditional or limited by memories and unresolved emotions, both of which limit us in our ability to forgive ourselves and others.

6. *What should I do if my mate asks for forgiveness but I am not ready to give this gift?*

If you are the one in the position of giving the gift of forgiveness, but you are not ready to truly give this gift freely and without reservation, you need to feel free to tell your mate that you are not ready at this time. Then you need to spend time with God alone, asking Him to reveal and remove the obstacles that keep you from being able to forgive. This is an act of the will, and more than anything else it is an act of obedience to God (Colossians 3:13). At the point where we yield our will in obedience to Him, He is able to bless us, and often the emotions—especially anger—that have kept us from forgiving will be transformed when we yield and act obediently by forgiving our spouse.

Scripture teaches us that holding onto anger creates a foot in the door for the Devil (Ephesians 4:26), and we are commanded to get rid of bitterness and anger, trading it in for kindness and forgiveness (Ephesians 4:31–32). Forgiving does not mean forgetting, and it does not mean that trust is reestablished. Only time will show whether or not your spouse has changed as a result of repentance. If you cannot come to the point of forgiving your spouse in prayer alone or with your spouse, seek wise counsel through a trusted Christian, such as a pastor, friend of the same sex, or counselor.

This exercise needs to be earnestly committed to God, with specific prayer for the Holy Spirit to bring the peace and genuine love that only God can provide. It might be helpful to read 1 Corinthians 13, praying for the attributes of love described in this chapter to be made real during this exercise.

Since love does not keep a record of wrongs, do not go into this exercise with the hope that your mate will confess things you are still holding against him or her. The focus should be on your own confession, and in keeping with this Scripture passage, you should narrow your focus to current events rather than the past. For the sake of limiting remembered offenses, start with only those wrongs done over the past two weeks. It is also helpful to start with wrongs that are the least offensive to your mate, and only move to deeper levels as both of you are comfortable with deeper levels of exposure and vulnerability. If you have practiced this particular exercise enough to feel comfortable dealing with unresolved issues needing forgiveness, go ahead and use this format if it is helpful to you. Some sins, as already mentioned above, may require counseling or other assistance beyond couple prayer as described in this manual.

While we were preparing this book, one of the things we experienced was an initial discomfort and anxiety because we did not know what to expect from each other. This can be helped by following the suggestion to prepare in advance by letting your mate know what actions, attitudes, or thoughts you will be asking their forgiveness for prior to actual prayer time together. Let your mate choose those items that he or she is most comfortable with and begin there. Allow your spouse to let you know if, when, and how he or she is planning to respond to any requests that you have made.

We habitually use notes to remind us of many things needing our attention, and for us it would probably help most to write down our mate's request if we need time to respond. We keep paper and pen handy during the exercises. Jotting down notes helps assure continuity in our prayer times, especially in following up on unfinished prayer needs.

As we engaged in the process of confession and forgiveness with each other, there was a sense of relief, release, and gratitude for each other, and a deeper sense of renewal and connectedness. Customarily, we ask forgiveness for the most obvious actions when they are committed. However, having a special exercise that focused on the Holy Spirit's revelation of attitudes, thoughts, and actions that were more hidden from one another gave us new insight into how our private sin still affects our spouse, causing unintentional harm to our marriage relationship as well as our relationship with God.

We hope that you both will be willing to trust God to guide you into this deep and richly rewarding area of spiritual intimacy, as it is the gateway to proceeding with the remaining exercises. To understand how this exercise acts as a gateway, review the next two exercises as they connect in sequence with this exercise. Exercises 9 and 10 are much less intimidating, but we do not believe that their intent will be met if exercises 6, 7, and 8 have not been completed.

Just as physical and emotional intimacy is not easy or automatic and improves with honest communication and practice, so too the spiritual nakedness necessary for true intimacy is not easy or automatic. But it improves with practice, especially when you ask the Holy Spirit to be your guide and covering in this process.

Remember to keep love as your priority, according to 1 Peter 4:8. Your focus is to be on loving each other, because it acts as a protective barrier, covering your sins. Love does not sweep wrongs under the rug, but it shelters and protects the persons involved by creating a safe environment to confront the truth through extending grace to one another.

Verse 9 in this same passage of Scripture calls us to extend hospitality to one another. In examining this word, we see that it contains the word *hospital*. Ideally, we think of a hospital as being a healing environment. Unless our marriages are "hospitals" in this same sense, we are lacking in hospitality and missing out on God's design for our marriages. They should be safe havens that promote life and growth—physically, emotionally, and spiritually.

Prayer Exercise 6

"Forgive us the wrongs we have done to each other, as we also forgive one another."
Ask and receive forgiveness from our Father and each other.

Purpose
- To restore your relationship to wholeness and holiness, both with God and your spouse
- To experience the cleansing and freeing effect of being released from the guilt of sin against your spouse and being restored to fellowship with both God and your spouse
- To experience being loved in spite of failing both God and your spouse

Helpful Materials
- Bible
- concordance
- notebook/paper and pens
- sacred music related to forgiveness that enhances prayer
- list of Scriptures related to forgiveness

Process
1. Taking turns in opening prayer, dedicate this prayer time to God. Ask Jesus to pour out his love to overflowing during this time so that love covers this exercise (1 Peter 4:8). Ask Jesus to cast out all fear of how your mate will respond (1 John 4:18). Ask the Holy Spirit to pour out his influence upon you, to empower you to ask for, receive, and be able to grant forgiveness.

2. In silence, wait for the Holy Spirit to reveal to you your sins against your spouse. You may have already confessed them to God and received His forgiveness. The primary purpose here is to ask and receive the gift of forgiveness from both God and your spouse for sins specifically related to each other. If you have already shared these sins with your spouse in preparation, as suggested in the introduction to this exercise, pray for the Holy Spirit to be with you now as you come together to engage in exchanging and receiving what God desires for both of you. Meditate on Jesus, the perfect model for forgiveness of undeserved hurt when he asked his Father to forgive those who were accusing and crucifying him, because they were ignorant of what they were doing and whom they were doing it to (Luke 23:34).

3. Take turns asking for and receiving forgiveness from both God and each other. It may be less threatening initially to start by asking God to forgive you, verbalizing this in front of your spouse, and then moving to asking forgiveness from your spouse as you

feel more comfortable. This helps to prepare your spouse for giving you the gift of forgiveness, having already witnessed your confession to God. Remember that this is not a score-keeping event. It is possible that one spouse needs more cleansing than the other, and therefore is in need of more gifts of forgiveness. It may be necessary to ask your spouse if he or she has been sinned against unknowingly by you, since we are not always aware of how our actions affect others. Use Scriptures related to forgiveness to formulate prayers over one another.

Here is an example of Scripture-based prayer:

Verse: If we tell God that we have wronged Him, and possibly others, and ask for His forgiveness, He will keep His word as a just God to forgive us and restore our standing with Him (1 John 1:9).

Prayer: "Father, I thank you for the gift of forgiveness that comes from confession—not just from you alone, but also from my spouse—and for making things right between us."

4. Taking at least one turn each, pray out a closing statement of thanks for the cleansing and restoration He has provided you in this prayer time.

5. Together or separately, complete the evaluation form and debrief with each other, focusing on what went well and what needs improvement. Don't skip the steps for discernment to evaluate the experience against Scripture as your guide, especially if words were spoken or feelings and thoughts arose that created doubt or confusion. Note on the evaluation form your plans for improvement for the next session. Using a notebook for journaling, take notes on significant aspects and insights that may be worth pursuing.

6. Set up the next appointment to meet with Jesus together in prayer. It may be helpful to read through the exercise ahead of time so that any advance preparation can be done prior to the appointment.

Prayer Exercise 6: Evaluation Form

1. Physical Experience:

    Plan for Improvement:

2. Emotional Experience:

    Plan for Improvement:

3. Spiritual Experience:

    Plan for Improvement:

4. Relationship Experience:

    Plan for Improvement:

5. Discernment of Experience:
    *   Does it glorify God?
    *   Does it conform to the doctrine of Christ?
    *   Does it conform to God's Word?
    *   Does it result in a character that is godly?
    *   Are your spouse or other Holy Spirit-filled believers in spiritual agreement?

    Plan for Improvement:

6. Next Appointment:

Preface to Prayer Exercise 7: Praying for Protection from Hard Testing

All of us have areas of weakness where, no matter how hard we try, we still fail to resist the temptation and fall short of God's standards and desires for us. We are only too aware of areas in which we lack the necessary willpower to consistently come out victorious. The purpose for asking your spouse to pray with you and for you regarding those areas is to establish a stronger position against the Enemy, Satan: He loves exploiting our weaknesses and then accusing us when we fail the tests set before us. There is strength in numbers, and not just in terms of physical force and mental strategy. More importantly in the area of temptations, there is strength when you allow another person to know your weaknesses and help you resist through accountability and prayer support.

As with the previous exercise, this one also requires transparency with one another. In order for this to be a safe experience, you must be able to trust each other to not pass judgment on one another. Nothing will undermine intimacy faster and more completely than being condemned for our failings and weaknesses by the person we trust them with.

It is very likely that you are both aware of at least some of each other's areas of weakness. Most habitual failings involve enough repeated behaviors that they are noticeable, especially to our spouses. However, there are secret failings that may not be known to your spouse. As in the previous exercise, you need to ask yourself certain questions regarding the impact of sharing a particular weakness with your spouse. If you are tempted and fail to resist in the areas of sexual fidelity (which includes pornography) or any major area that would destroy the trust base in your marriage, you may need to seek wise, mature Christian counsel prior to bringing this issue to your spouse. There may be areas you have already confessed, in which you have received forgiveness from your mate in exercise 6. If any of these areas need special attention because there have been repeated failings, these areas would be a good place to start.

While God does not tempt us (James 1:12–15), He does allow us our own free will. In that freedom, the Enemy is more than willing to take advantage of whatever we give him (1 Peter 5:8). In asking for prayer from your spouse, you are asking him or her to join together with you and Jesus to defeat both your own weakness to resist and the Enemy himself, who can only defeat you through your weaknesses (Romans 8:37–3; Romans 12:1–2, 21; John 16:33; 1 John 4:4).

Here, more than ever, when you are praying for your spouse, you need to resist the urge to use prayer language that comes across to your mate and God as moralistic, legalistic, judgmental, and self-righteous. This is also not the time for acting as a psychologist or counselor, giving advice or helping your mate "fix" the problem. While specific strategies to help your mate to succeed may be important, that discussion needs to be held apart from prayer time.

In prayer, you are enlisting the army of God to come to your spouse's aid, and Jesus, the commander in chief, has given you both all wisdom (James 1:5), all power (Acts 1:8; Ephesians 6:10), and all authority to defeat the Enemy (Luke 9:1). Ephesians 1:15–22 is a strategic prayer that encompasses all that God has given you to be complete in Jesus Christ, inheriting all that belongs to Jesus, including victory over every human weakness and your spiritual adversary, Satan. This is a good prayer to use for this exercise as well as the next one. Pray this covering over one another before tackling specific temptations and tests.

Scripture deals with two areas regarding temptation or testing. One area has already been addressed, namely resisting the Devil (and the temptation) and fleeing from evil as those situations come up. The other area deals with praying to be protected from tests that are too hard for us. Jesus asked His Father not to put him to the impossible test of crucifixion when he prayed in the garden of Gethsemane (Mark 14:32–42). Ultimately he yielded to what God wanted him to do, but only because he trusted his Father completely. He was already certain that his imminent death would result in resurrection according to the purposes and will of his Father (John 17:1–5), but the method of getting there was excruciating.

We can pray not to have specific trials and tests come our way, especially when we know we are too weak to gain the high spiritual ground and glorify our Father. We are asking to not be put to the test in areas where failure has been our repeated experience, or where we have no reason to believe that we can endure without succumbing to sin, even in the forms of fear, worry, and unbelief.

The Lord's Prayer, our model for prayer, gives us, his disciples, permission to pray against being led into temptation or testing. When God makes it clear that He will not remove the test, we are then asking to be able to pass it with flying colors under His banner of love.

As the partner praying for protection from and during situations that lead to temptations, your model for how to pray is contained in Scripture. Jesus prayed specifically for his disciples in John 17:6–19, dealt with Satan's temptation in the wilderness in Luke 3:1–13, and prayed for Peter regarding Satan's request to tempt him in Luke 22:31–32. Jesus gives us examples throughout his ministry years of how to pray and how to defeat the Enemy. When we appropriate his life by faith and walk it out, we have access to the power to live an undefeated life. Ephesians 6:1–21 is the manual for readiness in our war with the Enemy of our soul and life. It gives us all the specifics for putting on Christ himself so that our defeat by the Enemy is not possible.

As with the previous exercise, we both initially had some apprehension and anxiety, for this exercise required us to put ourselves in vulnerable positions. What we experienced as we took the risk was the Holy Spirit's presence through the gentleness, compassion, and mercy that enveloped us. With Jesus in our midst, we moved to a deeper level of both knowing and building up one another. Instead of being led to pray for the removal of situations, we found ourselves praying more for a change in responses to those situations. This is especially important in areas where it does not make sense for the situation itself to be removed.

An example of this was Wayne's frustration and anger when some of the computer software he uses failed to perform as expected. Because God gave him a job that requires this particular technology, praying for the computer or software to never fail did not meet the test of consistency with Scripture regarding how we are to respond in a "Murphy's Law" world (Genesis 3:17–19; Job 5:6–7; 1 Corinthians 10:13). By following the lead of the Holy Spirit, Wayne was able to get in touch with an old memory related to his "automatic" anger response to his computer, which damaged his Christ-conforming character. It had also affected Jan, because we work at home under the same roof. Jan then used this revelation from the Holy Spirit to pray support for Wayne in the area God was working on in conforming him to His image.

Jan's area of hard testing concerned the fear that Wayne would die much earlier than she would. Wayne was led to pray a twofold prayer that the situation would not occur and that Jan's fear would be removed. Jan needed to appropriate all of God's promises for her good in the present, and let go of the life-robbing nature of ungodly fear of the future (Jeremiah 29:11). By joining together in prayer against our common enemy, we were able to expand God's territory by reclaiming ground we had both abandoned to the enemy by giving in to ungodly anger and fear. The stage was then set for the courage to tackle the next exercise, where victory over strongholds would be obtained.

You need a way to follow up on areas and issues that come up during prayer time and may need ongoing prayer support. Especially in areas that are not one-time prayer needs, you need to check in with each other in a way that is comfortable for both of you. If you want your mate to check in with you, specifically ask for this. If you would rather ask your mate for his or her prayer support when you feel the need, be specific about this.

You may have very different needs and preferences regarding follow-up support. It is important during your evaluation and debriefing time to establish ways of working together that meet your unique needs and are comfortable for both of you. Be specific about what words are helpful and what words are not. "How are you doing?" is very different from "Are you staying away from your temptation today?" One is a question of general concern for overall well-being, while the second example is very pointed and may or may not be helpful, depending on the emotions it elicits.

There is a temptation, especially for men, to think that an expression of need is a sign of weakness. It is too costly to wait until the need is desperate before acknowledging one's need for prayers of support and protection. In our country, the price of freedom is eternal vigilance. Likewise, in the realm of spirit, the price of freedom from the Enemy's bondage is continual vigilance while we reside on earth.

Christ is eternally interceding for us before his Father's throne. For us and our marriages, the price of spiritual freedom is being willing to acknowledge our weak areas and let our spouse help carry that burden with us to Jesus, where we can join with him in a rope of three strands that is not easily broken (Ecclesiastes 4:9–12).

Prayer Exercise 7

"Do not lead us into hard testing."
Pray protection for each other.

Purpose
- To acknowledge the need for God's protection to keep you from sinning, especially against your spouse
- To pray for protection for your spouse without passing judgment
- To receive a protective prayer from your spouse without becoming defensive or resistant

Helpful Materials
- Bible
- concordance
- notebook/paper and pens
- sacred music relevant to the prayer exercise
- list of Scriptures that deal with temptation and testing

Process
1. Both taking brief turns, open this time of prayer with dedication to God, who is your ultimate guide, and who will not lead you astray. Let Jesus remind you that there is no temptation that he himself has not experienced (Hebrews 4:15), and there is no temptation so great that God will not give you a way out (1 Corinthians 10:13).

2. Wait in silence and ask the Holy Spirit to reveal to you your areas of temptation that need your spouse's prayer support to overcome. Make notes to assist you in the areas you feel safe to share with your spouse as well as other areas that you may need to deal with alone or with an accountability prayer partner of the same sex.

3. Take turns sharing a specific area of weakness where it is difficult or even impossible for you to resist succumbing to temptation. Pray for strength and protection for each other in your identified areas of weakness, including asking God to protect each of you by keeping you from those tests you are most likely to fail. Asking your spouse what he or she specifically needs and wants protection from will prevent the potential for judging and finger-pointing (Matthew 7:5). If you feel safe enough, ask your spouse to identify areas where you succumb but are blind to. Use Scriptures to formulate prayers as in previous exercises.

4. Taking at least one turn each, pray out a closing statement of thanks for this prayer time, knowing that God can keep you from stumbling into traps, providing you with all you need to avoid the snares set for you by the Evil One (Psalm 91).

5. Together or separately, complete the evaluation form and debrief with each other, focusing on what went well and what needs improvement. Don't skip the steps for discernment to evaluate the experience against Scripture as your guide, especially if words were spoken or feelings and thoughts arose that created doubt or confusion. Note on the evaluation form your plans for improvement for the next session. Using a notebook for journaling, take notes on significant aspects and insights that may be worth pursuing.

6. Set up the next appointment to meet with Jesus together in prayer. It may be helpful to read through the exercise ahead of time so that any advance preparation can be done prior to the appointment.

Prayer Exercise 7: Evaluation Form

1. Physical Experience:

    Plan for Improvement:

2. Emotional Experience:

    Plan for Improvement:

3. Spiritual Experience:

    Plan for Improvement:

4. Relationship Experience:

    Plan for Improvement:

5. Discernment of Experience:
    *   Does it glorify God?
    *   Does it conform to the doctrine of Christ?
    *   Does it conform to God's Word?
    *   Does it result in a character that is godly?
    *   Are your spouse or other Holy Spirit-filled believers in spiritual agreement?

    Plan for Improvement:

6. Next Appointment:

Preface to Prayer Exercise 8: Deliver Us from The Evil One

In previous exercises, you have moved into the most vulnerable areas of your marriage, coming face-to-face with Jesus and each other so that you could receive cleansing through confession and forgiveness. We hope that in this process you have also come to understand that God, your Father, *and* your mate want to join with you in defeating the Enemy.

Sometimes, even though God has clearly given us the means to avoid and escape temptations that would lead us to defeat, we seem unable to gain complete and total victory on a consistent basis in certain areas of our lives. Even when our spirit is willing, our human nature acts out (Matthew 6:41).

Paul wrote in Romans 7 about the human condition that we all must face. He described his own struggle with his heart's desire to do the will of God, and the inability of his human nature to cooperate. He even went so far as to cry out, "Who will free me from my own human nature, which is hell-bent on destruction?" The answer he gives is that God is his deliverer through Jesus Christ. The good news of the New Testament is that, through Jesus and his victory over Satan, we have the same power and authority over the Enemy that he has.

Jesus demonstrated how to resist temptation and Satan's attempt to deceive and confuse him by countering lies with Scripture, and then he ordered Satan to leave (Matthew 4:1–11). Christians are marked by the Holy Spirit as children belonging to God and cannot be possessed by Satan (2 Corinthians 1:20–22; Ephesians 1:13–14; Ephesians 4:30). As believers, our spirits are where God's Spirit dwells (1 Corinthians 3:16; Romans 8:9–11), and to the extent that we allow God to rule and reign in our lives, Satan has no place or power.

When God does not have total control of our lives, we give Satan the legal right to set up camp and lead us astray in those unyielded areas. In addition, all of us can also be oppressed by Satan and his demons, just as Paul was, even when we have not given legal ground to Satan through our own sin (Romans 7:14–25; 2 Corinthians 12:7–10). Jesus Christ has given us the authority to command the forces of evil to depart (Matthew 10:1; Luke 9:1; 10:17–19), just as he ordered Satan to depart.

At an earlier stage of prayer intimacy, you had the experience of praying blessings on one another, in accordance with God's will on earth. The focus of that exercise had to do with praying for God's best, as expressed in His promises of His goodness. The focus in this exercise is on deliverance from all evil that keeps our mate from experiencing God's blessings.

We have only to read Deuteronomy 11:26–28 to see the link between blessings and curses, defined here as the withholding of blessings. Clearly God has conditions for receiving

His blessings, and our failure to meet God's conditions results in negative consequences (Deuteronomy 30:19–20). While blessing someone invokes good things to befall them, our failure to meet God's standards sets us up for the negative result, which is that we reap what we sow (Galatians 6:7–9).

At the very least, our failure to be obedient will result in missing out on the blessing that would have accompanied obedience. Since every blessing is from our Father, God (James 1:17), only He has the power to grant or withhold blessings, dependent upon our status with Him. Likewise, only He has the power to allow or withhold permission from Satan to oppress His children (Job 1:6–12, 21; Job 2:10; John 9:1–3).

We may not always understand the reason for some of our afflictions or sufferings, and the book of Job eloquently deals with the ultimate question of why bad things happen to godly and righteous people. It is certainly appropriate to appeal to God to remove our afflictions and suffering, even if we do not understand the reason for them, and praying for each other to have God remove these evils is scriptural (James 5:13–16). However, we most often bring withholding of God's blessings on ourselves and others when we sin against Him, giving those negative consequences a legitimate reason to befall us. In order to pray that barriers to blessings be avoided or removed from one another, we must deal with the sin that sets the stage for God to withhold His blessings.

Until we are free from the Enemy's strongholds in our lives and in our marriage, we will not be able to receive all of the blessings that God has for us. The key to deliverance from the Evil One is in understanding what a stronghold is, how it leads to bondage and spiritual oppression, how the Enemy establishes it in our lives and marriage, and most importantly, how to tear it down.

In military terminology, a *stronghold* is a fortified place that is dominated by one side in the battle. When we are in God's stronghold, His fortress, we are perfectly safe from the Enemy, because God is stronger, and the Enemy cannot remove us or harm us in that stronghold (Psalm 61:1–4; Psalm 91). If we leave God's protection, which we do any time we are disobedient to our commander in chief, we are vulnerable to attack and being taken captive. Deliverance from an enemy is needed when we are held captive by an enemy that is stronger than we are, and we are therefore no longer free to run back to where we belong.

Jesus came to set us free from all that would keep us from what our Father, God, wants for us and yearns to give us, both individually and in our marriages. How then do we know when we have been taken captive by the Enemy? Any areas of our lives that are not submitted to God and do not reflect Christ are open for the Enemy to take advantage of. If we give the Enemy an opening for long enough, he will establish a stronghold and put up a fight to keep us from reclaiming that area of our life for God. At the point where you try to resist the Enemy to take back that ground in your life or in your marriage, the Enemy will likewise react, and you will generally have no trouble recognizing the stronghold.

An easy example is seen in the area of a habit that is displeasing to God, such as repeatedly breaking the law by exceeding the speed limit while driving. As long as we do not see that we are displeasing God, the Enemy does not have to do anything, because we are blind to the desire of God. Left to our own rebellion, which always leads to self-destruction, we will eventually reap what we sow through the logical and natural consequences of speeding, as well as the loss of blessings from God that come with obedience. At the point where God convicts us that breaking the law is displeasing to Him, the struggle over who we belong to begins. (Romans 13:1–7 and 1 Peter 2:11–16 deal with God's will for us concerning the laws of society.)

Satan does not need to do anything until we decide to whom we belong: God and the kingdom of light, truth, and life, or Satan and the kingdom of darkness, falsehood, and death. Once we commit our allegiance to God, war is declared against us by Satan and his forces of darkness. Scripture is clear that the victory already belongs to God who dwells in us, and we are equipped by God to resist and repel Satan, but we must choose to use His whole armor (Ephesians 6:10–18). The strongholds established by the Enemy in our life through our repeated rebellion against God begin to be torn down at the point where we admit that we have let the Enemy have victory over us in certain areas of our life, as in the example of willful speeding.

Lack of total submission to God always leaves room for the Enemy to move in, and lack of total submission weakens our ability to successfully resist temptation (James 4:6–10). Submission to God, followed by confession and repentance—which includes turning our life around and no longer doing that which is displeasing to God—destroys the stronghold of the Enemy and sets us free to run back to our Father's fortress.

Paul taught us in 2 Corinthians 10:3–5 that strongholds are in our minds. This Scripture refers to strongholds as wrongheaded arrogance and pride that resist and rebel against the knowledge of God. Clearly these strongholds are mental in nature, and verse 5 spells out the solution to the battle for the mind: taking every thought and conforming it to the character of Christ. This simply means that we need to ask, with every thought, whether this is a thought that Jesus would approve of, act on, or renounce.

While our freedom requires taking every thought and submitting it to Christ to prevent another stronghold of the Enemy from being set up in our lives, we need our mates to intercede for us along with Jesus, who intercedes for us continually (Hebrews 7:25). There are no shortcuts to staying free in Christ, just as there are no shortcuts to having the marriage that God desires for you and your mate.

Discipline of the mind starts and ends with evaluating every thought. It is a discipline that is humanly impossible to master completely. It is only by knowing the Truth, which is Jesus Christ revealed in God's living Word, and asking the Holy Spirit to speak to you when your thoughts are displeasing to your Father, that you can hope to stay free. Your marriage is hindered to whatever degree either one of you are not free in Christ, and Jesus pleads for you and your marriage continually, asking his Father to keep you free from the Evil One so that you may be blessed and not cursed (John 17; 1 John 2:1; Romans 8:26–27). God will not, however, violate our free will, and we must choose to serve Him alone if we want the freedom that only He can give.

If we are unable to stay turned around, facing God and demonstrating true repentance through our thoughts and actions, we need to call on the one who has all the authority over our enemy and ask Him for deliverance. We may need our mates to stand firm with us and use the authority Jesus has given us through the power of his name to renounce our sinful acts and the Enemy, and to command the Enemy's demonic forces to leave us. Once we are free of any demonic forces that may have taken up residence in the unsubmitted areas of our lives, we then need our mates more than ever to help us stay free.

A distinction needs to be made between God's curse on those who reject Him, and His discipline of His children in allowing us to reap what we sow due to our rebellion against what we know His will to be. For those of us who belong to Him, the proof of His love for His children is in His discipline of us (Hebrews 12:4–17). God's discipline should never be viewed as a curse. It is an act of love. Teaching us to walk in His ways is God's job as our Father. Those of us who belong to Him curse ourselves in the form of losing God's blessings. We bring about the very thing that God promises to those who do not walk in His ways.

Another distinction needs to be made between strongholds of the Enemy that we fall into through our own acts of rebellion, and those to which we fall prey through the effects of someone else's sin against us. It is not only our own actions against God that result in us cursing ourselves. Our *reactions* to the sin of others against us can result in losing God's blessings. The following accounts of our own experiences in doing this exercise should help illustrate this difference.

In doing this exercise, we found that we both had strongholds that are probably representative of the invisible kind. Without the Holy Spirit speaking to us in this prayer exercise, they would probably have remained undetected by us. Wayne was struggling with doubt and self-condemnation related to not fitting the "Christian model" for daily devotions, Scripture study, and prayer time. As the Holy Spirit spoke during this time, Wayne was able to recognize that his struggle was connected to an old childhood wound from a Sunday school teacher who labeled all of the boys in the class as "bad."

At that point, healing prayers, led by the Holy Spirit, broke the stronghold in his life that had resulted from an unhealed childhood wound. He was able to affirm who he is as God sees him, and who he is as God's child with his identity in Christ, rather than believing the condemning words of a fallible Sunday school teacher. The stronghold in his mind was created by allowing a lie of the Enemy to take firm root in his mind. Until he was able to see when and how the lie was planted, he was powerless to tear down that stronghold. He needed the Holy Spirit to reveal the source of the wound so that he could then forgive this person and ask God to forgive him for believing the lie. In addition, he needed to own the truth that God was not the source of condemnation (Romans 8:1) and that man-made "Christian models" are idols if we conform to them instead of Christ.

Jan was struggling with fear connected to being professionally attacked by a disgruntled, revenge-seeking, abusive parent of a child for whom she testified in court. Wayne's prayer, as led by the Holy Spirit, set her free. He prayed for God to break the chains with which the Enemy was binding Jan to this man through a professional relationship that had ended almost two years prior to doing this exercise.

It was exactly what needed to be prayed, as Jan instantly felt free and able to do more than stand on the intellectual truth that she is commanded not to fear (Isaiah 43:1–3). She had recognized that fear of what this man could do to her was sin, and that she lacked belief that God was in control, and she had no trouble confessing and renouncing it. But she could not stop the physical symptoms of anxiety that welled up inside of her whenever she received another notice or phone call regarding the very protracted grievance procedure.

Only the Holy Spirit could have revealed and severed the trauma bond that had been formed with this man. Once it was severed, Jan was freed not only to proclaim the truth that God is in control over her enemies, but to immediately feel the accompanying peace of that promise and stop reacting physically to the stress. Even though Jan conformed her mind to that of Christ by renouncing fear, the Enemy revealed his hiding place when she continued to physically react to his evil presence. It was not until the Holy Spirit revealed that a demon had attached itself to this bond between Jan and a human accuser, that the power and authority of Jesus Christ could be aimed at the right target.

Jan learned a valuable lesson in having her soul mate pray for her rather than trying to continue to fight the Enemy alone. Thinking that we should not burden others with our needs is a common stronghold of the mind in this culture of "rugged individualism," but it is not scriptural. Therefore, it is a lie as well as a sin of pride. Isolation is one of the Enemy's greatest means of keeping us captive, because it limits our ability to access all that God desires for us through the use of different gifts given to the body of Christ for the purpose of setting free and building up one another (1 Corinthians 12:14; 14:1).

These kinds of strongholds did not originate from personal sin that brought God's curses down upon either of us. Rather, they came from the power we handed over to the enemy in our minds at the point where we did not recognize and reject the Enemy's lies. Again, this demonstrates the truth of our mind as the battleground, and the importance of examining our thoughts to see where the lies of the Enemy have infiltrated.

This exercise, as was mentioned in the introduction to exercise 7, needs follow-up with your spouse. Once the Enemy has been ordered out of your life, the real battle to stay free begins, and more than ever you need prayer support and accountability. Scripture tells us that unless a house (our mind) that has been cleaned of demons *remains* clean and completely occupied by the Holy Spirit—which requires complete submission and conformity of your thought life to Jesus Christ—they will establish their dominion and their stronghold again (Matthew 12:43–45, 2 Peter 2:20–22). Either God establishes His stronghold in your life, or the Enemy is free to establish his.

Ask your spouse how he or she would like this follow-up support to occur. Doing it in a manner your spouse does not prefer might be perceived as nagging, pressure, or coercion. While this exercise is tough and engages you directly with the Enemy as you team under God's headship, there are all of those promises in Scripture regarding your assured victory. "Don't be discouraged, for Jesus has overcome all the evil of the world" (John 16:33, 1 John 5:4–5). This is our prayer for you.

After this, you will have completed the most demanding sessions: exercises 7 and 8. Then you will be ready to rest in God's mighty fortress and stronghold during the two remaining exercises and enjoy the fruits of His victory in your life and marriage (Psalm 56:13; 98:1; 116:1–9).

If, in doing this exercise, you encounter such resistance by the Enemy that freedom does not result (which may not happen immediately), you may need to bring other spirit-filled Christians who are familiar with deliverance ministry into this struggle. Be very careful, however, that both of you are in agreement about doing this. Ask help from those who are highly committed, Spirit-filled Christians, absolutely grounded in the Word of God and totally dependent on the Holy Spirit to reveal both truth and method for taking back surrendered ground.

Relying solely on learned or observed deliverance methods and rituals—while helpful, if fully grounded in God's Word—can limit God's creative power and lead to missed opportunities to hear the Holy Spirit's leading. We have spent years in healing and deliverance ministry and have learned to cling to God alone, as revealed in Scripture, and the leading of the Holy Spirit for His truth, presence, and power to heal and set free people who are caught by the Enemy. While we have studied and trained extensively in this area, we have firmly committed ourselves to using the discernment process presented in this book. God's ways of working are unique to each individual and situation, and He is infinitely creative, but His character never changes, and He does not contradict Himself as revealed in His Word.

Ultimately, the Bible is your source for all you need to be free in Christ Jesus, who came for the purpose of destroying the works of the Evil One (1 John 3:8), but it can sometimes be difficult to know how to apply Scripture. It is therefore helpful to seek wise counsel from those with experience in correctly applying it, especially in the area of deliverance. There are also many good books on the market dealing with how the Enemy operates and how to be delivered from evil, but you must test everything to see that it conforms to correct interpretation of Scripture.

Ask the Holy Spirit to lead you to what will help you best, whether it is enlisting others to pray with and for you, reading and gaining more information, or attending training in this area.

Prayer Exercise 8

"Deliver us from the Evil One."
Pray for deliverance for each other.

Purpose
- To identify strongholds in your life and marriage that keep you in bondage and spiritually oppressed
- To acknowledge your need to be delivered/freed from the evil and sin that so easily ensnare each of us (Hebrews 12:1–2)
- To pray for deliverance/freedom for your spouse without passing judgment
- To receive prayer from your spouse for deliverance/freedom without becoming defensive and resistant
- To learn to use the authority you have in Christ Jesus and to allow Jesus to show you the power of his name over all evil/sin

Helpful Materials
- Bible
- concordance
- notebook/paper and pens
- sacred music, especially praise music
- list of Scriptures that speak of deliverance from evil/Satan

Process
1. Praying in brief turns, dedicate this prayer time to God. Ask specifically for protection from the Enemy and for God's power to overcome your human nature and the Enemy's influence in your life and marriage.

2. In silence, focus on Jesus and the power given to you, his disciple, to stop the rebelliousness of your human nature and destroy Satan's desire to destroy you (1 John 3:8). Ask the Holy Spirit to show you areas where there is a lack of freedom to obey your Father, God, and all that He commands.

3. Take turns sharing areas of your life where you want complete freedom from the bondage/influence of your human nature and what is evil, asking your spouse to pray for those specific areas of weakness. Use Scripture as a base for prayers of deliverance. The book of Acts contains many verses where the name of Jesus was used with authority to empower words spoken to save, deliver, and heal the oppressed and sick. (See Acts 2:21; 2:38; 3:6; 3:16; 4:10; 4:12; 4:18; 4:30; 16:18; 19:13; 19:17.)

4. Read David's song of deliverance out loud together from either 2 Samuel 22 or Psalm 18. Taking at least one turn each, pray out a closing statement of thanks for victory gained over the Enemy during this prayer time.

5. Together or separately, complete the evaluation form and debrief with each other, focusing on what went well and what needs improvement. Don't skip the steps for discernment to evaluate the experience against Scripture as your guide, especially if words were spoken or feelings and thoughts arose that created doubt or confusion. Note on the evaluation form your plans for improvement for the next session. Using a notebook for journaling, take notes on significant aspects and insights that may be worth pursuing.

6. Set up the next appointment to meet with Jesus together in prayer. It may be helpful to read through the exercise ahead of time so that any advance preparation can be done prior to the appointment.

Prayer Exercise 8: Evaluation Form

1. Physical Experience:

   Plan for Improvement:

2. Emotional Experience:

   Plan for Improvement:

3. Spiritual Experience:

   Plan for Improvement:

4. Relationship Experience:

   Plan for Improvement:

5. Discernment of Experience:
   - Does it glorify God?
   - Does it conform to the doctrine of Christ?
   - Does it conform to God's Word?
   - Does it result in a character that is godly?
   - Are your spouse or other Holy Spirit-filled believers in spiritual agreement?

   Plan for Improvement:

6. Next Appointment:

Preface to Prayer Exercise 9: Deep Worship of God as Creator of Our Marriage

At this point in the Lord's Prayer, you have joined together with Jesus to petition your Father for needs, cleansed yourselves and your relationship through the tough work of forgiveness, defeated the Enemy through reclaiming lost ground, and even claimed new ground. The hardest work is over. You are now at a place where you can come into the throne room and just worship your Father for what He has given you both in your marriage. The energy needed to spiritually consummate your marriage is spent, and this is a time of "afterglow," where you can both bask in the love of your Creator, God, who has seen you yield to His highest desire for your union.

This exercise is meant to be a triumphant declaration that acknowledges the Father's kingdom, power, and glory, realized through Jesus Christ's headship over your marriage.

In coming to understand what you are praising God for in your marriage, it is helpful to see the parallel mysteries of marriage, as God designed and ordained it, and the church, as God designed and ordained it (Ephesians 5:18–33). The mystery of both institutions is contained in the transformation that results from two becoming one, where neither are the same as before, and the union itself is greater than the sum of the two individuals.

Christ, through the Holy Spirit, is the transformer of both marriage and the church, because he is ordained to be head of both, as God designed and created both. The fifteenth chapter of John's gospel contains the transformation that occurs when you are united with Christ: you experience God's love just as He does, and you love one another just as He loves you. Jesus revealed that he wants you to remain united with him so that your joy may be complete, so that you can be his friends, and so that the love he channels through you will spill out to the world. Your marriage was never designed by God to be an end in itself, but rather a means to this end: to glorify Him and enjoy Him forever, even now on this earth.

God, our Creator, first gave the command to be fruitful and multiply within the institution of marriage in Genesis 1:27–28. While He was obviously referring to physical offspring, we believe there is also scriptural support for His command including the more important spiritual fruit that Jesus talked about in John 15:1–17. Your marriage and the church are both instituted by your Creator for the purpose of advancing His kingdom on this earth. You cannot do this in your own strength, because God desires that the glory be given to Him alone. If you could do the work that only God can do, you would not need Him and would therefore not give Him the credit. Scripture is clear about where all good and perfect gifts come from (James 1:17).

Scripture is also clear about where the power comes from that allows you to be used by God to do His work and will (2 Samuel 22:33). This exercise is meant to engage the two of you together with Jesus as the acknowledged head of your marriage to lift praise and honor to God your Father alone. Scripture speaks about each of us having different gifts and functions in both marriage and in the church (Romans 12:4–8; 1 Corinthians 12:4–27).

You do not need to think strictly in terms of actual work that you do side-by-side, but rather those things that would not be possible without your spouse as a team member. God created us to first need Him and then to need one another in order to do the work that is glorifying to Him. Praises in this exercise should focus on "we" rather than "you" or "me." You are thanking your Father for what He has done corporately through the two of you, rather than thanking Him for the character and attributes He has caused to develop in yourself or your mate.

As with the other exercises, it is helpful to prepare in advance to facilitate a smoother praise and worship time. Ask the Holy Spirit to reveal what God has done in and through your marriage itself, and specifically things that he has done because of the two of you together. In our case, we are frequently in prayer ministry as a couple, so it is relatively easy to identify His use of our marriage in this way. Other ways that He has glorified Himself through our marriage is in restoring His vision for Christian marriage and family to both us and our children, as Jan had been married previously to a Christian man who did not exemplify God's design for husband or father to either Jan or her children by that marriage.

Think in terms of what God has produced in your marriage that neither one of you can claim as God's work in you alone as individuals. If you have children, they are an obvious product of both of you physically, emotionally, and spiritually. If you have supported the efforts of one another to do the work to which God has called you individually, this is another area where God has brought about His work using the two of you together.

Wayne does professional work that is very different from the professional work Jan does. We both recognize that neither one of us could trade places to do those jobs, because God has gifted us very differently, but they would be impossible to do well without the full and ongoing support of one another. Even tasks around the house require different gifts and abilities, but they would not be as doable or even as pleasing to God if we did not support one another.

We have spent a great deal of time trying to be good stewards of the house that God has given us, and while Jan is better at using a caulking gun than Wayne, she needs him to place and support the ladder for her for in places she cannot reach without it. A praise to the Father for the purpose of this exercise might be worded thus: "Thank you, Father, for creating a team out of the two of us for the purpose of being good caretakers of this house. Thank you for the harmony between the two of us when we need each other and work together." Notice that the emphasis is on something God has created between the *two of you*, such as harmony, rather than individual attributes such as "her patience" or "his physical strength."

If you cannot relate to any characteristics in your marriage as being the product of God's work in both of you, you may need to return to exercise 2. The evidences of a God-created and Christ-headed marriage are fruit of the Spirit in both of you. In other words, your marriage will bring out the best in both of you. There should be evidence of both of you growing in Christlike wholeness as individuals, even if the areas of growth and rates of growth are different for each of you. We are all called individually to pursue personal wholeness and holiness, and the degree to which we individually conform to Christlikeness will be the degree to which our marriages reflect corporate wholeness and holiness.

We did not experience strong emotions with this exercise, and when we debriefed, we realized that the presence of a lack of strong emotions is not a good indicator of how meaningful prayer time is. It also makes sense that after the intensity of the previous exercises, where much energy may be needed to deal with tough issues, this exercise is not expected to generate the "heat of passion" that is created with intense engagement with each other.

We also found ourselves without words to adequately express all that God had created through our yielding this marriage to Him, so we found ourselves suspended in a state of silent wonder and awe. This made step 4 seem anticlimactic and unnecessary, so we skipped it.

Prayer Exercise 9

"Your kingdom, your power, and your glory belong to you forever."
Worship God deeply as the creator of our marriage.

Purpose
- To praise God's design for marriage, acknowledging the mystery (Ephesians 5:18–33)
- To give glory and honor to God through acknowledgment of His Son's headship (John 15:7–8)
- To see the sacredness of marriage in a new way through the blood of Christ (1 Corinthians 6:20)
- To thank Jesus for taking headship (Matthew 11:28–30)

Helpful Materials
- Bible
- concordance
- notebook/paper and pens
- sacred music that enhances prayer
- list of Scriptures related to Christ as head of the church, which includes your marriage

Process
1. Taking turns, dedicate this time of worship to God, the Father, maker of heaven and earth. Thank Him for creating man and woman, united as one through marriage. Ask Jesus to give you a new awareness of the impact of his headship on your marriage. Ask the Holy Spirit to worship with you, making your praises acceptable to your heavenly Father.

2. In silence, ask the Holy Spirit to reveal to you the gifts you have received as a couple. This differs from the earlier exercise that focused on each other's individual gifts. Focus on what God has created in the two of you together. Take notes to facilitate prayer together.

3. Taking turns, give thanks to God for what He has revealed to you regarding the gift of your marriage. Use Scriptures to formulate prayers as in previous exercises.

4. Taking at least one turn each, pray out a closing statement of deep thanks for what God has shown you during this prayer time. If this step seems anticlimactic, feel free to skip it, but check with your mate to be sure you have finished step 3.

5. Together or separately, complete the evaluation form and debrief with each other, focusing on what went well and what needs improvement. Don't skip the steps for discernment to evaluate the experience against Scripture as your guide, especially if words were spoken or feelings and thoughts arose that created doubt or confusion. Note on the evaluation form your plans for improvement for the next session. Using a notebook for journaling, take notes on significant aspects and insights that may be worth pursuing.

6. Set up the next appointment to meet with Jesus together in prayer. It may be helpful to read through the exercise ahead of time so that any advance preparation can be done prior to the appointment.

Prayer Exercise 9: Evaluation Form

1. Physical Experience:

   Plan for Improvement:

2. Emotional Experience:

   Plan for Improvement:

3. Spiritual Experience:

   Plan for Improvement:

4. Relationship Experience:

   Plan for Improvement:

5. Discernment of Experience:
   - Does it glorify God?
   - Does it conform to the doctrine of Christ?
   - Does it conform to God's Word?
   - Does it result in a character that is godly?
   - Are your spouse or other Holy Spirit-filled believers in spiritual agreement?

   Plan for Improvement:

6. Next Appointment:

Preface to Prayer Exercise 10: Deep Agreement with Christ as Head of Our Marriage

The Lord's Prayer, while ending with the word *amen*, does not mean that reaching this stage in couple prayer means "the end." When we end our prayers with this word out of habit and without understanding, the implication is that, because it is said at the end, the word must somehow mean "the end." In fact, the word is of Hebrew origin and means "certainly," and it is a statement expressing agreement or approval.

The purpose of this exercise is to experience the deep love that God has for your marriage. Just as in the previous exercise, this one is meant to allow you to be in a state of rest and relaxation after the hard work of coming to climax in your spiritual union through the work involved in exercises 4 through 8. This is a time to rest secure in the certainty of God's love and promises for your marriage, just as Scripture declares in 2 Corinthians 1:20. When we have Christ as the head of our marriage, we can claim God's incredible *yes* for us and rest assured that God is for us (Romans 8:31).

We urge you, as with all the other exercises, to prepare in advance by reading the exercise, looking up Scriptures cited, and using a concordance for Scripture study to facilitate your prayer time. Most of the particular Scriptures given in each exercise were revealed to us as we actually did the exercises, since we were the original subjects of these exercises. During this exercise especially, Jan was flooded with God's Word during step 2, where she was seeking the Holy Spirit to take her to a deep place of understanding her Father's love for our marriage.

Scripture after Scripture flooded out, and she wrote the words down to look up the actual references and contexts later. This is important in the discernment process, because the Holy Spirit promises to reveal all truth (John 16:13), but we are commanded to test the spirits through the Word of God (1 John 4:1–6). We cannot emphasize enough how important knowing God's living Word is, both in the person of Jesus Christ and through God-inspired and infallible Scripture (2 Timothy 3:16).

Wayne, on the other hand, felt somewhat disconnected during this step, because he could not stay in the present focus of this exercise. He kept thinking about "what comes next," since we originally planned to end the exercises with this one. He got a vision of a dumbbell (two equal weights attached by a short bar), and in our debriefing, we sought God for an interpretation of this image. Wayne came to realize that this image represented the need for balance between the two mates, sustained in unity in the middle by Jesus Christ.

This then became the springboard for exercise 11, regarding the two questions proposed by the dumbbell vision: "How do you support each other's uniqueness?" and "How do you sustain the unity needed to nourish each person's uniqueness?" Just as the uncoupling process in physical intimacy is not meant to be the uncoupling of the marriage, exercise 10 is not the end of your spiritual intimacy as a couple.

Exercise 11 is meant to be a template for moving forward with one another in other aspects of spiritual intimacy in prayer, where the focus is still on the two of you but moves beyond the spiritual "marriage bed" that the first ten exercises established.

Prayer Exercise 10

"Amen, so be it."
Agree deeply with Christ for our marriage.

Purpose
- To come to a new level of understanding that "a threefold cord is not easily broken" (Ecclesiastes 4:12)
- To covenant anew with Christ for your marriage: "Apart from me you can do nothing" (John 15:5)
- To agree with Christ that the purpose of your marriage is the same as his, which is to bring all glory and honor to our Father (John 12:27–28)

Helpful Materials
- Bible
- concordance
- notebook/paper and pens
- sacred music related to marriage
- list of Scriptures related to marriage as the act of two becoming one
- candles that can be used to rededicate your marriage through the symbolic act of each of you lighting a separate candle, and both of you joining to light a third candle
- elements of communion, with one piece of bread to be broken and shared, and one cup to be drunk from

Process
1. Taking turns, open this prayer time with a brief dedication to God your Father, God's Son, Jesus, and the Holy Spirit. Thank God for binding you and your spouse together with Christ as your head.

2. Ask the Holy Spirit to take you to a deep place of understanding your Father's complete love for your marriage. Women, Jesus is the bridegroom, and you and your spouse are his bride, a scriptural concept that women connect with more easily than men. Men, please note the chapter on gender differences, which includes how to relate to Christ from a male perspective. Christ is your commander in chief, and you and your mate are two of his soldiers. Take notes, if this is helpful.

3. Taking turns, speak out what the Holy Spirit gives you from this deep well of His love for your marriage. Take notes for further remembering and savoring. Use Scriptures to formulate prayers as in previous exercises.

4. Taking at least one turn each, pray out a closing statement of thanks for this prayer time. If it seems agreeable to both of you, use the candles and communion as a rededication ceremony. This is also a good time to ask your Father to help you to keep your commitment to pray together as part of your dedication of your marriage to Him. Thank Him for what He has given you in your journey into deeper spiritual intimacy with Jesus and each other.

5. Together or separately, complete the evaluation form and debrief with each other, focusing on what went well and what needs improvement. Don't skip the steps for discernment to evaluate the experience against Scripture as your guide, especially if words were spoken or feelings and thoughts arose that created doubt or confusion. Note on the evaluation form your plans for improvement for the next session. Using a notebook for journaling, take notes on significant aspects and insights that may be worth pursuing.

6. Set up the next appointment to meet with Jesus together in prayer. It may be helpful to read through the exercise ahead of time so that any advance preparation can be done prior to the appointment.

Prayer Exercise 10: Evaluation Form

1. Physical Experience:

    Plan for Improvement:

2. Emotional Experience:

    Plan for Improvement:

3. Spiritual Experience:

    Plan for Improvement:

4. Relationship Experience:

    Plan for Improvement:

5. Discernment of Experience:
    *   Does it glorify God?
    *   Does it conform to the doctrine of Christ?
    *   Does it conform to God's Word?
    *   Does it result in a character that is godly?
    *   Are your spouse or other Holy Spirit-filled believers in spiritual agreement?

    Plan for Improvement:

6. Next Appointment:

Preface to Prayer Exercise 11: Planting Your Feet in the Garden

If you have completed all the exercises so far, you have hopefully arrived at your destination: God's garden, where there is deep and intimate fellowship between the three of you. Our experience is that, unless you commit to staying in the garden, just as you committed to using this workbook for your journey to the garden, your most intimate prayer life together will likely end here.

For some of you, it will be sufficient to have completed the journey. This does not mean that you won't continue to pray together, but it will probably lack the intensity and intimacy of what you have experienced within a committed time and specific focus on each other. We were highly motivated to use the exercises as we wrote them—and again when we facilitated a group using the materials. We loved seeing how God would reveal Himself and speak to us in new ways every time we did the exercises, even though we were repeating them over and over to refine them. Our prayer life together grew to new heights in the process of writing this book, and we enjoyed just praying for each other without our focus being scattered by the needs of others.

But we are well aware that over time the priority for intimate prayer is easily lost in the daily bustle of life, and it is easy to resort to shorter, easier formats for prayer together. Just as physical intimacy can diminish over time, so can emotional and spiritual intimacy. All three forms require a commitment of time and energy by both of you that may not seem to be in ready supply. God is not the one who has shifted His priorities: He is the one always waiting for us, longing to draw us and keep us and our marriages in His garden, walking and talking with Him. For those of you who want to remain in the garden with your mate in intimate prayer, the following suggestions, which include another exercise, may help you.

1. Make sure that you are also making time for emotional and physical intimacy. These areas are as important to the health and growth of your marriage as spiritual intimacy, and they tend to suffer the same loss without committed time. Set a "date night" once a week, and make it a priority. It may very well lead to greater emotional intimacy followed by greater physical intimacy.

2. Use any of the exercises again, in any order that seems appropriate. Agree ahead of time what exercise you will be using so that you both can prepare, just as you did as you moved through the book. This book provides a road map and format for moving you into greater prayer intimacy with God and your spouse, but it is undoubtedly not the only way to achieve this.

   However, if you change the format, focus, or structure of your prayer time, make sure your spouse is aware of any changes and agrees to them. We had an experience with one of the exercises in which Wayne wanted to spontaneously experiment to see what would happen, as he is a scientific researcher by training and occupation. It fell flat when Jan was not in on his alteration, and this led to confusion, hurt, and an abrupt end to the prayer time.

Regardless of the format, unless your prayer practice is centered on building up one another, other agendas can quickly creep in that will cause hurt and broken trust.

3. Ask God to call you back to His garden when you and/or your spouse have roamed away from the desire to intimately pray together for one another. Give it the same priority for a solution that you would if physical and/or emotional intimacy in your marriage were lacking.

4. Covenant with another couple or keep your original covenant group together to help motivate you and keep you accountable. (See Appendix 3. Remember, you do not have to share intimate details of your prayer time. The purpose of the group is to support and motivate each other to complete the prayer time.)

Have a weekly meeting to discuss what has worked and what has not worked for you over the past week within the context of your marriage. Use the information to focus your plans for change where needed, and also to focus your prayer time individually and together. (Use the Conflict Resolution Script on pages 11-12 if you have trouble articulating your needs.) It is a good idea to write down the content of this meeting to use for prayer and accountability.

Early on in our marriage, we set a weekly time to discuss the status of our relationship, just between the two of us, and called it our "State of the Union Meeting." (We had a separate weekly family meeting, where our children could discuss the pluses and minuses of their week.) We used the results as a springboard to continue what was working well and to implement changes that would address deficiencies.

Initially, we didn't think to use these same results to guide a specific prayer time together. But later—based on the dumbbell vision Wayne received at the end of exercise 10—we realized that the results of "State of the Union Meetings" could be used during couple prayer to bring unmet individual needs and praises within the marriage before God in structured prayer, just like the earlier exercises.

While Exercise 5 focuses on asking God to meet your spouse's needs generally, this final exercise focuses on your mate's individual uniqueness and desires as they are specifically impacted by your marriage, for better or worse. It is possible that Exercise 5 addressed some of these issues—if there was enough trust to ask your spouse to pray for what you are lacking because of the state of your marriage. But exercise 11 is designed to be used after a meeting where the two of you focus only on your relationship and how it impacts each of you so that possible solutions can be generated, and so that there are no surprises during this prayer exercise.

This is also the last exercise because a greater level of vulnerability and trust is needed to be able to express to our spouse that the marriage itself is posing a problem for us. We all have wants and desires as individuals that sometimes conflict within our marriage, and we may need to adjust expectations in our quest to attain and maintain unity. However, we should not lose our God-created, individual uniqueness with God-given desires and needs in the process.

A relatively benign example from our marriage is friction created by the fact that Wayne works at home, while Jan is retired and generally home during the day. If she wants to have friends over for her charity-knitting group, something needs to be worked out to prevent the noise from keeping Wayne from his work. Wayne doesn't want to prevent her from meaningful activities and the use of their home, and Jan doesn't want to interfere with his need for quiet when he is working. He came up with his own solution by obtaining ear protectors designed for use on a shooting range, which block out the noise.

Sometimes though, we have godly desires that cannot be met as a result of our marriage. Jan loves kids, and after retiring from her profession as a children's therapist, she would have loved to have been a foster parent for young children or have young grandkids spend whole summers at their home. However, because Wayne works at home and needs a calm and quiet environment both during work and to relax when not working (his personality type is a strong preference for introversion), either one of these options would have been highly disruptive and stressful. Instead, Jan met this desire through being a Girl Scout leader, tutoring, and having grandkids over for shorter periods of time.

A fulfilling marriage requires balancing the necessities and wishes of our spouse against our own, held together by the overarching desire of each of us for the best interest of our spouse. It is Christ who is the head of Christian marriage, holding in balance the requirements and longings of both spouses through his perfect model as the sacrificial servant and his command to love each other in the same way that he has loved us (John 13:34). While we aspire to be Christlike toward our mates, the journey will have inevitable struggles as we bump up against our own needs and wants, even when they are godly.

This final exercise is designed to be used following a "State of the Union Meeting," where the past week of your journey is reviewed with your spouse.

Prayer Exercise 11

"God said, 'It is not good for the man I created to be alone in my garden. I will create a helper and intimate companion for him'" (Genesis 2:18–25).
Plant your feet in the garden.

Purpose
- To facilitate ongoing prayer with your mate based on what is working for each of you (a praise) and what is not working for each of you (a want or need) within your relationship, as identified during your weekly "State of the Union Meeting," outlined in the introduction
- To continue to build up your mate and your marriage, designed by God for you to come alongside as unique individuals and helpers to one another (Genesis 2:18)
- To remain in spiritual communion with your Father and your mate, taking to His throne of grace every praise and every need concerning each of you within your marriage
- To hold on to God's promise in Psalm 37:4, that He will give you your heart's desire if you first find your joy and satisfaction in relationship with Him

Helpful Materials
- Bible
- concordance
- notebook/paper and pens
- the results of your "State of the Union Meeting"
- sacred music that enhances prayer
- list of Scriptures related to this exercise

Process
1. Praying in turn, dedicate this prayer time to God, your Creator and the creator of your marriage; and to Jesus Christ, your Head and the head of your marriage.

2. In silence, focus on God as the only one who can perfectly meet your every need. Acknowledge that expecting your spouse to meet all of your needs—or yourself to meet all of your spouse's needs—is not realistic or what God expects of your marriage. Using your notes from your weekly meeting, ask the Holy Spirit to reveal to you your real needs and God-given desires. Ask for discernment as to whether your felt needs and wishes are in line with what God desires for your marriage and for you individually. If you and your mate were not able to find a solution to a need or want

expressed during your "State of the Union Meeting," ask the Holy Spirit to reveal a real, workable solution. Take notes, if it will help, during prayer time with your spouse.

3. Take turns sharing an unmet or met need, based on what you expressed and worked out in your "State of the Union Meeting," and have your spouse send up a petition for your unmet need or a praise for what is working well for you. Include physical, emotional, and spiritual needs for petitions and praises. If you worked out a solution to a need your mate expressed during your weekly meeting, and it is something you need to do differently, ask your mate to pray over you for the ability to make the change. Keep notes regarding your mate's needs for prayer support as well as any solutions that you are responsible for so that you can hold yourself accountable. Use Scriptures that speak of met and unmet needs and desires and turn them into praises or petitions for each other.

4. Taking at least one turn each, close out your prayer time with praise to God, who created marriage because He believes that a unique man needs a unique woman as a helper by his side, and to reaffirm Jesus Christ as the head of your marriage.

5. Together or separately, complete the evaluation form and debrief with each other, focusing on what went well and what needs improvement. Don't skip the steps for discernment to evaluate the experience against Scripture as your guide, especially if words were spoken or feelings and thoughts arose that created doubt or confusion. Note on the evaluation form your plans for improvement for the next session. Using a notebook for journaling, take notes on significant aspects and insights that may be worth pursuing.

6. Set up the next appointment to meet with Jesus together in prayer. It is helpful to agree on what type of prayer you are planning to have, since this is the last exercise in this book. If it is an exercise from this book, read through the exercise ahead of time so that any advance preparation can be done prior to the appointment. If using a different format, make sure that you are both aware of any advanced preparation needed.

Prayer Exercise 11: Evaluation Form

1. Physical Experience:

   Plan for Improvement:

2. Emotional Experience:

   Plan for Improvement:

3. Spiritual Experience:

   Plan for Improvement:

4. Relationship Experience:

   Plan for Improvement:

5. Discernment of Experience:
   - Does it glorify God?
   - Does it conform to the doctrine of Christ?
   - Does it conform to God's Word?
   - Does it result in a character that is godly?
   - Are your spouse or other Holy Spirit-filled believers in spiritual agreement?

   Plan for Improvement:

6. Next Appointment:

Chapter 4

Parting Thoughts

It is our prayer that your journey was worth the effort you made and the risks you took to grow in spiritual intimacy with your mate, walking and talking with each other and God in new and creative ways. Your marriage is God's creative masterpiece, just as you are individually. Spending time in His garden places you in His master studio, allowing Him to mold and make you and your marriage into His image and His heart's desire. You are both planted by God to be trees of righteousness, bearing His fruit at the right time, not withering away but prospering in all that you do, so that He is glorified (Isaiah 61:3, Psalm 1:3).

We hope that you both will desire to stay in God's garden with Him in a three-way conversation, talking and listening, planted firmly and growing. If this book has helped draw you and your spouse into greater spiritual intimacy through prayer together for each other, as it did for us in creating and using it, all the glory and honor belong to God alone. May you be the richer for it emotionally as well, knowing that both your spouse and God your Father are there for you, building you up and centering you in their love.

Appendix 1

Prayer Survey for Married Couples

1. Sex: _____ Male _____Female

2. Do you and your spouse pray together (just the two of you and at times other than meals)? _____ Yes _____ No

3. Would you like to pray with your spouse? _____ Yes _____ No

   If so, what are your reasons for wanting to pray together?

4. If you don't pray with your spouse but would like to, what are the hindrances or obstacles to doing so?

5. Are any of the obstacles to praying with your spouse related to discomfort or uneasiness on the part of either one or both of you? _____ Yes _____ No

   Is this discomfort mainly _____ yours _____ your spouse's _____ both of you?

6. If you feel there are some obstacles related to your own discomfort or uneasiness, how would you describe these?

7. If you feel there are some obstacles related to your spouse's discomfort or uneasiness, what do you think these are?

8. Do you think praying with your spouse would

   a _____ improve your relationship?   c. _____ not change your relationship in any significant way?

   b. _____ add more stress to your relationship?

9. What would you like to see happen in your marriage, yourself, and in your spouse as a result of praying together?

In your marriage:

In yourself:

In your spouse:

10. If you do pray with your spouse, how often do you pray together?

a. _____ Daily

d. _____ once a month

b. _____ 2–3 times a week

e. _____ less than once a month

c. _____ once a week

11. When you pray together, how long do you usually spend in prayer?

a. _____ 5 minutes or less

d. _____ 20–30 minutes

b. _____ 5–10 minutes

e. _____ more than 30 minutes

c. _____ 10–20 minutes

12. When do you usually pray together? (check all that apply)

a. _____ suppertime

d. _____ a special time set aside just for prayer

b. _____ other mealtime

c. _____ just before going to bed

e. _____ whenever we can find the time

f. _____ whenever there is something special we need to pray about

g. _____ only when there is a crisis

h. _____ other (specify) _____

13. How would you describe your experience of praying with your spouse? (Check all that apply.)

a. _____ boring

b. _____ an obligation

c. _____ threatening

d. _____ spiritually fulfilling

e. _____ a spiritual adventure

f. _____ makes me feel vulnerable

g. _____ a cornerstone of our marriage

h. _____ frustrating

i. _____ something I look forward to

j. _____ sometimes scary or intimidating

k. _____ calm and peaceful

l. _____ brings us closer

m. _____ other (specify) _____

14. If your experience of praying with your spouse is positive on the whole, what has made it that way?

15. If your experience of praying with your spouse has not been as positive as you would like, what has prevented it from being a more positive experience?

16. In prayer times with your spouse, have you ever felt (check all that apply):

a. _____ lectured to

b. _____ put down or belittled

c. _____ manipulated

d. _____ coerced, forced, or pressured

e. _____ your prayer was regarded as unimportant

f. _____ your spouse was only
praying with you to keep you
happy

g. _____ other (specify)_____

17. What goals or expectations do you have regarding your prayer times with your spouse?

18. When you pray with your spouse, do you pray for expressed or felt needs you each may
have? _____ Yes _____ No

19. Do you pray for other people or concerns outside of those in your immediate family?
_____ Yes _____ No

20. When praying with your spouse, have you ever felt a deep sense of the Holy Spirit's
presence? _____ Yes _____ No _____ Unsure

If yes, how would you describe this experience?

21. What do you think explains the difference between the time(s) when you felt the presence
of the Holy Spirit and those when you did not feel His presence?

Appendix 2

Wedding Vows

This traditional wedding vow is originally from the Anglican Church *Book of Common Prayer*, 1549:

"I _____ take you _____, to be my lawful wife/husband, to have and to hold from this day forward, for better or for worse, for richer or poorer, in sickness and in health, to love and to cherish, until death do us part, according to God's holy ordinance."

Appendix 3

Helps for a Couples Prayer Group

1. The purpose of the group is to provide encouragement, support, and accountability so that participants carry out their commitments to themselves, their spouses, and the group to complete this workbook, with a focus on sharing and helping one another on their journey toward couple prayer intimacy.

2. When starting a group for this book:
   - The group can be as small as two couples.
   - Limit the group to no more than six couples. Any more will decrease participation.
   - Seek other couples that are motivated by the book topic of intimate couples prayer, willing to purchase the books, willing to read and do the exercises, and will be able to attend the group for twelve weeks.
   - Decide on the date/time/place/length of meeting (one hour minimum).
   - Decide if refreshments will be provided and by whom. If you choose to do this, save it until the end of the meeting so it doesn't sidetrack the purpose of the group, and factor in additional time.
   - Decide who will facilitate the meetings. This task can be rotated each week.
   - Make sure that everybody in the group knows where to obtain the book, and clarify the need to read the introductory material as far as the first prayer exercise before the first meeting.

3. Expectations of members of the group:
   - Obtain a copy of the book and read the introductory material as far as the first prayer exercise before the first meeting.
   - Attend the group for twelve weeks.
   - Come to each meeting on time.
   - Come prepared by having completed the assignment for the week. If, after reading the assignment for the week, you and/or your mate are not comfortable with completing the prayer exercise, at least use a previous prayer exercise that you were both comfortable with, including evaluation and debriefing.
   - Participate in discussion of the book content for each week, and be willing to share thoughts related to the prayer exercise and evaluation of the experience. Intimate details are not necessary. Share only what you and your spouse are comfortable with, including obstacles to your prayer time that interrupted or prevented you from doing

the weekly exercise so that the group can help you troubleshoot the problem and encourage you on your journey.

- Maintain confidentiality regarding what is shared in the group.

4. Facilitator role and expectations:
   - The facilitator's role is to help the group function smoothly in its intended purpose and to be a participating member of the group.
   - Open the meeting on time, and end it on time. If you choose, open and/or end with a brief prayer.
   - At the first meeting, open with introductions that include reasons for wanting to read this book and join this group. (This should take about five minutes.) Expectations for participating should be reviewed. (Instruct the group to refer to this page to read them. All members should already have a copy of the book and should have read the materials up to the introduction to the first exercise.)
   - Discussion of the material follows, with each member taking turns sharing their thoughts on each section. In order to ensure everybody's participation, it is easiest to just go around in a circle, one member at a time. As facilitator, you need to ensure that only one person speaks at a time, that interruptions are stopped, and that the discussion stays on topic. You need to be willing to intervene if a member is dominating the time when it is their turn to speak. Remind them gently that the time for the group is limited and everybody needs a chance to speak, so the group needs to move on.
   - Announce the week's assignment, which will be to read and try the first prayer exercise, including the introduction and completing the evaluation form.
   - For the remaining eleven meetings, spend no more than about five minutes for social time at the beginning of the meetings. Keep track of time so that you start and end on time.
   - For exercises 1–11, ask the following discussion questions, allowing each member to speak by going around in a circle:
     1. What are your impressions of the assigned material?
     2. What are you comfortable sharing about your prayer exercise experience? (Refer to your evaluation form.)
     3. How have you been impacted by trying this exercise?
     4. Do any of you need the group to help you in any way to complete the assignments? If yes, how?
     5. Are there any other comments or questions related to the materials?
   - For the final meeting (exercise 11), ask questions 1–3, and add the following questions:
     1. How did this book impact your marriage and your prayer life with your spouse?
     2. How did this group impact you?

3. What did you like or dislike about this book that hasn't already been discussed?
4. How many of you want to continue in this group to support continuing intimate prayer with your spouse like you have done to complete this workbook?

About the Authors

Jan and Wayne have published in their respective professions of social work and sociology.

Jan has coauthored church ministry programs for children of divorce and has done freelance writing.

Wayne is currently writing a book summarizing forty years of research on the Myers-Briggs Type Indicator.

They reside in Buena Vista, Colorado.